Entrepreneurs + Mentors =

SUCCESS

22 CONVINCING STORIES

Entrepreneurs + Mentors =

SUCCESS

22 CONVINCING STORIES

By Barnett C. Helzberg Jr.

with Deborah Shouse

ROCKHILL
B O O K S

KANSAS CITY, MISSOURI

Entrepreneurs + Mentors =
SUCCESS

22 CONVINCING STORIES

Copyright © 2012 by Barnett C. Helzberg Jr.

Proceeds from this book will be donated to HEMP.

Edited by Donna Martin
Designed by Brian Grubb

Grateful acknowledgment to Bruce Mathews for his photos of mentees.

Published by Rockhill Books,
An imprint of The Kansas City Star Co.
1719 Grand Blvd., Kansas City,
Missouri 64108

ISBN: 978-1-61169-046-0
Library of Congress Control Number: 2012936158

Printed in the United States of America by
Walsworth Publishing Co. Inc., Marceline, Missouri

This book is dedicated to our mentors, whose
spirit of giving has helped so many entrepreneurs
create jobs and success. Without your generosity,
these stories would not exist.

Mentee class of 2005 with their mentors.

*Monthly meeting at the
Ewing Marion Kauffman Foundation.*

ACKNOWLEDGMENTS

Tennyson wrote, "I am a part of all that I have met."

All of us have been the beneficiaries of our experiences and the wonderful people we have known.

I must acknowledge my number one mentor and amazing bride, Shirley Bush Helzberg; my parents' influence; my many mentors, especially Ewing Kauffman, Ted Cohn, and Barney Karbank; brothers Richard and Charles; my fine sons Barnett III and Bush Helzberg, their loving wives Jen and Jamie, and my seven miraculous and beautiful grandchildren who have so enriched my life; and the many marvelous people at Helzberg Diamonds who taught me so much.

My special thanks for unlimited patience and putting up with my attitude of, "There is no good writing; there is good rewriting!" to Deborah Shouse, who did a marvelous job gaining understanding of HEMP culture and interviewing some of our wonderful HEMPers; Tom Eblen, retired journalism professor, University of Kansas, and unindicted co-conspirator at my wedding; Donna Martin, my very patient and forgiving editor; Brian Grubb, my highly creative and open-minded designer; Debbie Murphy, my long-suffering and indispensable associate at the Helzberg Foundation; Christina Friederichs, our wonderful HEMP managing director, who keeps our program running smoothly; Doug Weaver, of the Kansas City Star publishing arm, who was so very helpful and understanding of my goals; and Bob Litan, who named this book after we looked at dozens of potential titles.

This book was inspired by seventeen years of wonderful, generous, and caring mentors and mentees and their amazing accomplishments in creating success for their companies and increasing opportunities for their associates.

Here's hoping you will find these folks as wise and inspiring as I have!

– BARNETT C. HELZBERG JR.

CONTENTS

x **Preface**

Part 1: Growing HEMP: How a Successful Mentoring Program Found Its Way

2 **Chapter 1** Creating HEMP

5 **Chapter 2** Navigating New Territory

8 **Chapter 3** HEMP: The Fiber of Community

Part II: HEMP Helps: Case Studies from Mentees

14 **Chapter 4** A Crash Course in Small Business

16 **Chapter 5** Turning Challenges into Opportunities

16 • *Laura Lee Jones and LionShare Marketing: Growing the Entrepreneur, Then the Company*

21 • *Joe Lieberman and SPIDERtel: Untangling an Acquisition*

25 • *Mary Lou Jacoby and Warehouse 1: Getting Focused and Financially Sound*

29 **Chapter 6** Refusing to Give up

29 • *Gary Short and Sys-Tek: Building Confidence and Rebuilding Business*

34 • *Dan McDougal and Dredge America: Dredging up Good Communications and Human Relations*

39 • *Laura Laiben and the Culinary Center of Kansas City: Cooking up Creative Business Solutions*

44 • *Ernie Ketcham and Galvmet Steel and HVAC Supplies: Steeling Himself for Change*

48 • *Elizabeth Amirahmadi and International | Architects | Atelier: Architect of Her Own Company*

53 **Chapter 7** Transforming the Family Business

53 • *Missy Love and Alaskan Fur: Fashioning Financial Savvy*

57 • *Deuce Livers and Livers Bronze: Taking the Bronze and Strengthening the Family Business*

62 • *Jason Collene and Collene Concrete: Building a Focused Foundation*

66 **Chapter 8** Defining a Niche and Filling It

66 • *Joe Runyan and Hangers Cleaners: Cleaning up the Profitability*

71 • *Neal Sharma and Digital Evolution Group: Making the Most of Peers and Mentors*

75 • *Rick Krska and InkCycle: Inking into the Black*

80 • *Dave Cacioppo and Emfluence: Targeting Technology and Customer Service*

84 • *Emily Voth and Indigo Wild: Cleaning Up with Fun and Healthy Products*

89 **Chapter 9** Following the Entrepreneurial Dream

89 • *Danny O'Neill and the Rise of the Roasterie: Brewing Success*

96 • *James Davis and Davis Safety Supply: Taking Business to the Next Level*

100 • *Michelle Robin and Your Wellness Connection: Growing through Becoming the UDM (Ultimate Decision Maker)*

104 • *Andrew Homoly and Homoly Construction: Growing a Business the HEMP Way*

108 • *Leanne Cofield and Visage, Inc: A Quick Course in Business and Promotions*

112 **Chapter 10** Becoming a Nonprofit Entrepreneur

112 • *Kay Julian and the National Multiple Sclerosis Society: Mid America Chapter: Engaging the Board*

Part III: Creating a Culture of Connection

118 **Chapter 11** Matchmaking

122 **Chapter 12** Creating Advisory Boards

124 **Chapter 13** Steering HEMP toward Change

127 **Chapter 14** Creating a Mentee Boot Camp

129 **Chapter 15** The Economics of HEMP: Moving toward Self-Sustainability

134 **Chapter 16** Starting an Entrepreneurial Mentoring Program

142 **HEMP Dictionary**

145 **Reading List**

146 **Index**

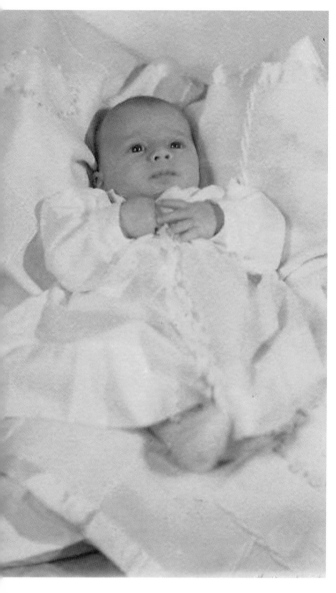

A little history.

In 1933, just in time to get a deduction, I was born into a most interesting family.

My mother was a journalist, a book lover, and wonderful raconteur. My father was a family man and a great merchant, who had taken the family's tiny jewelry business over at age fifteen when his father had a stroke and one brother was at war and the other in dental school. This was before the age of women running businesses, which I'm sure Aunt Elsie could have done very well.

Our mother and father believed in exposing my two brothers, Charles and Richard, and me to the business at very young ages. We were always encouraged to be open and creative. I found out that I especially loved advertising and created ads that my folks, of course, always thought were wonderful.

My middle brother, Charles, and I had some entrepreneurial experiences. These included printing of a neighborhood newspaper (on gelatin!), repackaging and reselling our doctor's skin prescription (which we named Dint), selling address signs for homes as door-to-door salesmen, and forming a photo development business from our basement darkroom.

Our great business adventures included going to the Kansas City, Kansas, Helzberg store and offices to price-tag merchandise and even sit in on meetings. Summers and school vacations were spent working at our stores.

I started out being a runner, taking merchandise and escorting the customer to the lower level credit department of our 1100 Walnut, downtown Kansas City, Missouri, store. As a very timid young man, I found this trying.

When I later got the green light to become a salesman, I found my niche and competed very effectively with older and highly experienced salespeople. At one point almost to the embarrassment of my dad!

Dad was a highly creative merchant. In many cases he went against the conventional wisdom in the industry, creating Certified Perfect Diamonds, a non-negotiating pricing policy, the Teenage Watch Club, the Dime a Day Sterling Silver Club, and other unique ideas including institutional advertising showing no merchandise at all.

After receiving a Bachelor of Business Administration degree from the University of Michigan in 1956, I went into the business as a diamond buyer. I found merchandising fascinating, especially in the area of learning what would sell and what would not, and sometimes being very wrong on potential successes of new items!

Later I became assistant to the president through the blessings of nepotism. When my dad became ill when I was age twenty-nine, he told me he wanted me to be the president of the company. I readily accepted. Of course, I asked him if I would really be president and he backed me all the way, sometimes to the detriment of the company.

One of his favorite quotes was, "The only place where fools may learn is the school of experience!"

I had a great deal of fun in the business, including some lucky strokes like the creation of the "I Am Loved®" button. When I was walking on air in 1967 and got engaged to a beautiful young lady named Shirley Bush, I created an advertisement saying, "Give her a Certified Perfect diamond ($50 to $5,000) or Give her an 'I Am Loved®' button (no charge, of course), but tell her she's loved."

Helzberg's announces the

I AM LOVED

**button
(to give you a choice)**

Academically speaking, your problem is a simple one: How to tell her you love her.

Of course, there's the standard answer, still supreme. The exclusive Certified Perfect diamond ($50 to $5000 at Helzbergs).

And now we've invented another way. The "I AM LOVED" button (also at Helzberg's. And there's no charge.).

It'll never replace the Helzberg's Certified Perfect diamond. But it might give you another week to bolster your courage.

Helzberg's
Middle West's Largest Jewelers

1100 Walnut / Plaza / Metcalf South / Prairie Village / Mission / 7th and Minnesota / Independence / North Kansas City
Every Helzberg Certified Perfect Diamond is certified and guaranteed by us to be of fine color, perfect in cut and proportion, and free from imperfection of any kind.
Copyright 1967, Helzberg's Diamond Shops, Inc.

As luck would have it, the one-month I Am Loved® campaign became a raging success, and about fifty million buttons and forty-five years later, Helzberg Diamonds is still giving away free buttons!

I always claim I never worked a day in my life due to the joy of business and wonderful people with whom I have worked.

Actually, we had some very bad times in the sixties due to some very faulty decisions. We had pulled out of a lease with one of the first covered mall shopping centers and were saddled with a number of dying downtown stores and were operating licensed jewelry departments in discount stores.

Due to poor financial results, one of my most valuable learning experiences happened when the First National Bank of Kansas City told us they were unwilling to make a loan on January 11 after we had mailed our suppliers' checks out on January 10.

Fortunately we had another bank, the Security National Bank of Kansas City, Kansas. The Breidenthal family had always backed my dad through thick and thin and backed his sons as well. That was a day that could have lived in infamy!

With the opening of the Metcalf South mall store in Overland Park, Kansas, in 1967, we realized that our future was in malls. Although we were late to the party, we were able to recover and redirect our efforts.

We closed 38 of our 39 existing units, and by 1995 we had 143 stores. When it came time to sell the business, we were fortunate enough to sell the company to Warren Buffett's Berkshire Hathaway.

Years earlier I had attended a seminar by the Young Presidents' Organization (YPO) and met Ewing Marion Kauffman ("Mr. K"), the founder of Marion Laboratories and owner of the Kansas City Royals. We had good chemistry and he told me to "drop by the office" when I returned to Kansas City.

That started a mentoring relationship that lasted twenty-three years until he passed away. When I thanked him one day he said, "That's okay, you'll help someone someday." That certainly helped inspire the creation of the Helzberg Entrepreneurial Mentoring Program (HEMP).

Another part of my inspiration was my repeated exposure to two of my dad's most trusted advisers, Max Skeer, a noted Kansas City real estate man, and his esteemed attorney, Arthur "Tim" Mag. These examples showed me the value of asking and listening to others.

In June of 1995 we had a meeting in the basement of our home with a number of Kansas City leaders about the idea of an entrepreneurial mentoring program. All but one was very positive.

As I write this, HEMP is seventeen years old and has gone through many changes, improvements, and mid-course corrections. Hopefully this will always continue.

The purpose of this book is to encourage entrepreneurs (who are open to mentoring) to select a mentor and also become part of a networking group. It may also encourage the startup of entrepreneurial mentoring programs.

This book includes interviews of some of our HEMP heroes by Deborah Shouse (in which I am referred to as Barnett). They are not the famous and hopefully not the infamous but are no less heroes than the entrepreneurs most books are written about!

I hope these stories of entrepreneurial winners provide inspiration and wisdom as well as enjoyment.

*Tribal leaders Ray Pitman,
Chuck Hoffman, and Barnett.*

PART

1

GROWING HEMP:

HOW A SUCCESSFUL
MENTORING PROGRAM
FOUND ITS WAY

*Barnett and industrial psychologist and
founding mentor Harvey Thomas.*

CHAPTER 10

CREATING HEMP

Chuck Hoffman,
president, CKC Trucking Company and Hoffman Management Company

Ted Cohn,
Theodore Cohn Consultant

Dr. Harvey Thomas,
Thomas & Associates

Henry Bloch,
cofounder, H&R Block

Bill Eddy,
dean emeritus, UMKC Bloch School of Business

"I don't see how it's going to work," Chuck Hoffman, president, CKC Trucking Company and Hoffman Management Company, said to Barnett, after being told about the mentoring idea. "I don't see how you'll get high-powered business people to volunteer their time and energy."

For several years, in the early 1990s, Barnett talked to Kansas City business leaders about creating a formal mentoring program that would match business leaders with upcoming entrepreneurs. Some liked the idea, and some thought the concept would never work. Barnett had benefited from his networking and connections with the many successful people in the Young Presidents' Organization (YPO). But it was focused on larger companies with larger resources. Barnett visualized a program with smaller companies and lesser costs to the members.

"Barnett knew from personal experience that entrepreneurs rarely have the broad managerial skills or experience to handle all the functions of a growing business," says Barnett's consultant and friend, Ted Cohn of Theodore Cohn Consultant. "He also understood that the entrepreneur who was a great developer may need help in financing and marketing. He felt that a mentoring organization could help growing businesses."

Dr. Harvey Thomas, Thomas & Associates, was integral in helping define and develop the mentoring concept. Harvey had worked with both Marion Laboratories and Helzberg Diamonds in his role as a human resource and training consultant, and he strongly believed in the power of mentoring.

Questionnaires were sent to a number of Kansas City leaders asking what they thought of such a program. Morton Sosland, of Sosland Publishing, wrote back that it was not possible to create such an organization because of its dependence on personal chemistry.

Barnett still believed it could be done.

Just Doing It

In May 1995, Helzberg Diamonds (by then 143 jewelry stores) was sold to Warren Buffett's Berkshire Hathaway, a publicly traded holding company. This freed up Barnett's time.

In that same year, Barnett was invited to lunch with three forward-thinking men: Rich Davis, physician and creator of KC Masterpiece Barbecue Sauce; Bill Eddy, dean of Bloch Business School at the University of Missouri-Kansas City (UMKC); and Bill French, vice chancellor for university advancement, UMKC. They invited Barnett to orchestrate a gala for the school. He declined, explaining he really wasn't good at that sort of thing.

"Maybe you could start an entrepreneurial mentoring program," Bill Eddy said.

As a life-long educator in management and business schools, Bill knew that having a mentor was an important element in the success of business executives.

Barnett went home, looked in the mirror and said, "Either quit talking about it or do it."

HEMP: From Concept to Reality

First came the task of soliciting prospective mentors, business people with deep experience and name recognition. One was Henry Bloch, cofounder of H&R Block. Henry's beautiful wife was Barnett's first cousin.

"Will you participate in this new mentoring program?" Barnett Helzberg asked.

"How can I turn you down?" Henry replied.

"Henry added much-needed credibility," Barnett says. "We listed every mentor on the

The late Barney Karbank, who christened HEMP a cult, with Shirley Bush Helzberg.

letterhead and fortunately Henry was at the top of the alphabet! He was an important catalyst for the program."

In June, the first mentor meeting was held in Barnett's basement.

Harvey Thomas moderated the session, which included some of Kansas City's most important civic leaders.

"I assume you've all had mentors in your lives," Harvey said to the group.

They began sharing mentoring stories, which ranged from learning the right clothes to wear to understanding the best time of day to call on people.

One man told the story of a trusted colleague being very blunt with him: "Before you approach the bank for a loan, wash your hands," the colleague said. "You smell like raw meat!" The man had been helping his father part-time in the family butcher shop.

Barney Karbank, of blessed memory, who was a leading Kansas City real estate entrepreneur, talked about the business and social challenges he had faced, going through life disabled by polio. His moving personal story inspired others to openly share their own issues and challenges. By the end of the meeting, there was a palpable sense of connection and community.

"We were walking on air," Harvey recalls.

The vision of the program was coming into being.

The University of Missouri-Kansas City (UMKC) agreed to be a sponsor. The Kauffman Foundation also offered a sponsorship and start-up funding. The Helzberg Foundation contributed additional funding. The Helzberg Entrepreneurial Mentoring Program (HEMP) was born.

Chuck Hoffman lost the bet that HEMP wouldn't work and earned his princess crown!

P.S. Naysayers Become Yaysayers

Two years after HEMP began, Morton Sosland called with congratulations, eager to hear what was going on with the program. Chuck Hoffman got deeply involved with the program. He has served as mentor, president, and board member.

CHAPTER 2

NAVIGATING NEW TERRITORY

How did HEMP manage to create an effective mentoring system and a vibrant entrepreneurial community? What started out as an experiment is now a well-documented program. Early on, the HEMP developers realized they were in new territory.

"That required us to experiment," says Walt Rychlewski, an early HEMP mentor and professor of entrepreneurship at the Bloch School of Business & School of Computing and Engineering, UMKC. "We tried different things, noticing what didn't work and why. Then we focused on what was working. By giving ourselves permission to try a lot of things, we weren't worried about failure."

Putting the Worst Foot Forward

Walt Rychlewski,
professor at the Bloch School of Business & School of Computing and Engineering, UMKC

Walt knew first hand the power of mentoring. Throughout his career, from engineer to entrepreneur, and from professor to dean, mentors had guided him to success. So when Barnett Helzberg invited Walt to be part of developing HEMP, Walt was instantly enthusiastic.

"I felt that HEMP was a great way to formalize the mentoring process," he says.

As a mentor with HEMP, Walt always shares his own personal story with his mentees.

"I want people to realize how much they can benefit from putting their worst foot forward, even though it may be initially uncomfortable," he says.

Walt's Story

As an engineer, Walt worked with companies that automated manufacturing processes. In 1979, two psychologists with PhDs came to him to discuss automating the process for administering and scoring psychological tests. Walt had studied artificial intelligence and the development of expert system software and his wife had studied psychological testing. He consulted her and created the initial program. A few months later, he partnered with the psychologists to start a company offering such services.

The new product filled a market need and Walt suddenly found himself running a thriving business.

"It was both exciting and overwhelming to build a business based on a new technology that almost instantly transformed the testing industry," he says.

Walt was comfortable with the technological innovations, but he had much to learn about the complexities of forming, financing, and operating a high-tech business. Fortunately, he connected with legal, financial, sales, and product development experts who patiently guided the fledgling leadership team.

When the company was a year old, a visionary venture capitalist invested in it. The board was celebrating the investment when one of Walt's partners said to the new investor, "We're glad we have you on board, because we don't know if Walt can handle running the company."

Walt was stunned, chagrined, and embarrassed. He worried the lack of confidence would concern the investor. Walt also felt the company might not survive a leadership change.

A Mentor Saves the Day

Later that evening, the investor took Walt out for a drink.

Walt's stomach was in knots as he waited for the investor to criticize or fire him.

But the investor said, "I have complete confidence in you. I will personally help you address your shortcomings and leverage your strengths."

The investor became Walt's mentor. Walt's desire to learn and his willingness to acknowledge his weak points made him an ideal mentee.

"I was always questioning and when I got advice, I acted on it," Walt says. "I showed my mentor what I'd done with his guidance and that encouraged him to offer more feedback and share more ideas."

Some of the issues they discussed over the months included ways Walt could:

- Become a better manager.
- Finance and run a company.
- Handle hiring issues more effectively.
- Manage the expectation of his investors.
- Create an agenda and run a board meeting.

Through that relationship and the lessons learned, Walt became a successful entrepreneur.

Beauty and the Beasts – Molly Proffer, Don Proffer, and Walt Rychlewski.

"My mentor had a tremendous impact on me, my family, and my life," Walt says.

"He taught me that entrepreneurship is a team sport. Few people have the skills to effectively run a company alone. My mentor taught me to form a management team that had a common vision and the combined expertise to offset personal weaknesses and meet all challenges."

Inaugurating the Mentoring Program: Henry Bloch

Henry Bloch agreed to be one of the first mentors.

"I had never heard of anything like HEMP," Henry said.

He agreed to be one of HEMP's first mentors because:

- He thought it would be interesting to meet fellow entrepreneurs and learn their stories.
- He had been through a lot of struggles building his business, and Henry thought he could help others on their entrepreneurial journey.
- He was curious to see how mentoring worked and thought he would enjoy the process.

Three Components of a Good Mentor

Though Henry Bloch never had a mentor of his own, he intuitively understood the components of mentoring. For him, three components were key to creating a strong mentoring relationship.

Credibility. "You have to be convincing," Henry says. "It helps to have a strong reputation, so the mentee can believe you. If I was mentoring a professional football player, he would never believe me. But our company grew from two people to over a hundred thousand, so I have some credibility in developing a business."

Interest. "You have to be genuinely interested in the mentee as a person and also interested in the company."

Generosity. "Mentoring is volunteer work and you have to enjoy it and want to help. The mentee's appreciation and success is your pay."

Sharing Wisdom and Building Success

Danny O'Neill, founder of the Roasterie, was Henry's first mentee.

Henry identified with Danny's penchant for treating work associates like family and with his intense work ethic. Henry's low-key suggestions helped Danny shape his business and keep his sanity. Some of the ideas included:

- As the business grows, the employees may need to become more specialized.
- Taking a vacation is imperative. You think you need to be on the job all the time, but it works the other way. You need trustworthy people to run the business while you're gone.
- Keep at it; there are no shortcuts.
- The customer is your boss. Even if they're wrong, they're right, because in their mind, they're right.

The Mentoring Advice Keeps Giving

Danny pictures their mentoring relationship like a grandson and grandfather sitting on the front porch. The grandfather imparts wisdom to the grandson, as the time is right. For Danny, Henry's wisdom is timeless and still guides him. Though Danny and Henry ended their formal mentoring relationship after three years, Henry's advice continues to influence Danny's business decisions.

Henry Bloch autographs copies of his book at the retreat.

CHAPTER 3

HEMP: THE FIBER OF COMMUNITY

HEMP's official mascot, Corby, before an exciting HEMP meeting.

Enough of these meetings!

Building a Community

Christina Friederichs, *HEMP managing director*

A dog wanders into the room, wearing a HEMP t-shirt. He lies down near the president of the board as the HEMP managing director offers people the HEMP signature green drink. People are laughing as someone rings a cowbell, calling the meeting to order. Before the brainstorming session gets under way, the HEMPers go around the table, introducing themselves and state one reason they appreciate the program. This kind of comfortable and positive atmosphere helps build the culture of connection that is at the heart of HEMP.

"In building the culture, we established the confidential nature of our conversations and then created a sense of family, belonging, and fun," says Christina Friederichs, HEMP managing director. "Our meetings, while focused on entrepreneurship, also offer a welcome release from the seriousness of business."

Advantages of a Community

Early on, HEMP founders realized that entrepreneurs were hungry for a peer group to discuss business issues. So HEMP began developing monthly meetings.

"The networking before and after the meeting is often as valuable as the meeting itself," says Bill Eddy.

To add an educational component and further deepen the sense of community, HEMP also created a series of opportunities.

Walt Rychlewski's scientific cowbell test.

Linda Gill Taylor, Tom McDonnell, Doug Klink, Bill Eddy, and Barnett at an early HEMP meeting.

These include:

Lunch with the Big Guy (LWTBG)—HEMPers have a chance to discuss pressing business issues with a small group of peers in a conversation that Barnett facilitates.

Lunch with the Big Guy (LWTBG). Host Laura Lee Jones presents a gift to the Big Guy.

Educational Sessions—The ongoing educational programs cover five major categories: Sales, Marketing, Finance, Operations, and People issues, such as leadership, management, and human resources.

Retreats—These one-day getaways offer the opportunity to learn from business leaders about topics of mutual interest.

Bush Helzberg moderates the financial panel at the retreat.

Networking—Every HEMP gathering is planned with networking time. In addition, a great deal of networking takes place at annual social events such as Celebrate HEMP and Schmooze Fest, as well as Thirsty Thursdays where members meet at a local restaurant at the end of the day.

John Vandewalle, Dan Nilsen, and Mike O'Malley smile for the birdie.

Mark Zecy, forum trainer Sue Hesse, Alton Hagen, and Linda Gill Taylor.

Forums—At an early meeting, Bill Eddy divided mentees into breakout sessions. The energy of those groups was so empowering that someone suggested they keep meeting. Thus began the forums, five to ten people that meet monthly and share issues, from business to family problems, with absolute confidentiality.

SWOT Teams—A SWOT (Strength, Weaknesses, Opportunities, and Threats) Team consists of selected HEMPers who meet as a group with the requesting mentee to address current concerns.

Society of Fellows—Initially, HEMP was a three-year program. At the end of the period, many relationships were so strong that the mentees did not want to leave the organization. This loyalty inspired the creation of the Society of Fellows. Participation as a Fellow includes the following.

- Invitation to HEMP events.
- Special opportunities and programs designed specifically for Fellows.
- Continued mentoring opportunities.
- Annual contributions to the program.

Renee McDougal presents a hiring seminar at Fellows breakfast club.

Counselors—Individuals who are not currently matched with a HEMP mentee, but have a wealth of experience they are willing to share with others in HEMP. They may be willing to serve on an as-needed basis for a limited period of time or be included in the ongoing pool of available mentors.

Advisory Boards—A small continuing group of unrelated advisers without an ax to grind who are willing to be brutally honest with the HEMPer.

On the following pages are some of the stories of how the mentor/mentee relationships in HEMP have helped entrepreneurs.

Starting Your Own Mentoring Relationship

Look for respected business people whom you admire. Learn more about those who might be interested in mentoring.

- Let people know you're looking for a mentor.
- Start networking, going to lunch with people, using social media, visiting online interest groups. "Network among friends or in business organizations to find a senior experienced person who has a calling to help people," Bill Eddy advises. "Consider retired business people who would enjoy helping someone else."
- Ask for what you want. Be specific in describing your needs.

Mentors Deborah Young and Bill Eddy solve world problems.

Doug and Cheryl Klink at HEMP's first retreat at the Elms Hotel in Excelsior Springs, Missouri.

Peter Long hugs his Build-a-Bear friend at the HEMP retreat.

Bill Hartnett,
vice president Business Development, Harvest Productions.

Advancing through Retreats

"It has to be fun." That's the first rule of any HEMP event, program, or retreat.

As the leader of the programming committee, Bill Hartnett, vice president, Business Development, Harvest Productions, designs events and retreats that are sustainable and repeatable, so a committee can recreate them.

When planning a program or retreat, Bill considers:

Take-Home Value. The program must have information entrepreneurs can inject right into their businesses.

Confidentiality and Openness. "As entrepreneurs, we are always selling, promoting, and projecting confidence because that's how we stay alive," Bill says. "But we need to be able to discuss our areas of weakness."

The programs are opportunities to learn and talk about issues.

Social Connections. Every event includes a time for participants to talk and network. That helps build the sense of community and encourages that open culture of connection that draws people to the organization.

"That's part of the culture," Bill says. "That bond and trust allows us to put our worst foot forward. We then learn faster, because we don't have to pretend we know something we don't."

2

HEMP HELPS:

CASE STUDIES FROM MENTEES

Treasured mentor, the late Barney Karbank, counsels a mentee.

CHAPTER 4

A CRASH COURSE IN SMALL BUSINESS

These case studies are a crash course in small business. They illustrate some key concepts that entrepreneurs have learned through the HEMP mentoring process.

Every business is unique, yet entrepreneurs often struggle with similar issues.

These stories plunge you into the intense world of small business problem-solving, dealing with issues ranging from financials, personnel and customer service, marketing, communications, and more. No matter what your profession, you'll be informed and inspired by the vulnerability, determination, adaptability, and creativity that are characteristic of the true entrepreneur.

Defining the Entrepreneurial Mentee

"We wanted the entrepreneurs to come into HEMP when they're being forced to delegate," says Chuck Hoffman. "That's a critical time because entrepreneurs feel their business is their baby and no one can run it like they can. Yet, if entrepreneurs don't learn to delegate and develop a more formal organization, they're limiting their company growth."

Chuck Hoffman,
president, CKC Trucking Company and Hoffman Management Company

Mentor Deborah Young shares the spotlight with her mentee, the late Nancy Smith.

Mentor Ed Nelson with his mentee Mike Pasley.

The criteria for the mentees include:

- A million dollars or more in annual volume.
- A minimum of five full-time employees.
- Reasonably good financials. (HEMP's goal is to build companies, not to save them.)
- A record of integrity inside and outside their organization.
- A passion for their business.
- Openness to new ideas.
- Willingness to help others.

Bill Eddy,
dean emeritus,
UMKC Bloch School
of Business

Defining Mentors

"As we developed HEMP, we worked to define the role of the mentor," says Bill Eddy. "There's a tendency for people to want to be the expert. That wasn't what we had in mind. We wanted the mentor to ask, 'Am I a good listener? Am I willing to let the mentee make mistakes?'"

HEMP developed a list of specifications and best practices for mentors. The ideal mentor is a veteran business owner or top-level executive with the following qualities:

- Willingness to openly share business knowledge – both successes and failures.
- Willingness to meet with the mentee a minimum of two times per month the first year and one time per month each year thereafter.
- Commitment to attend 50 percent of networking programs, including the annual retreat.
- Commitment to attend all joint mentor/mentee meetings and all mentor-only meetings.

The HEMP volunteer mentors claim they learn as much from the mentees as the mentees learn from them!

Laura Lee Jones and LionShare Marketing:

GROWING THE ENTREPRENEUR, THEN THE COMPANY

"You have two weeks to sign this noncompete contract. If you don't, you're fired."

Laura Lee Jones stared at her boss in disbelief. She had been running his small Kansas City-based marketing company for about five years. During the ten years she had been there, she had grown the business. Her commission-based salary had moved to a level that made her boss uncomfortable.

Despite all her contributions and the company's successes, her boss refused to discuss the situation. He escorted her from the building. Devastated, Laura Lee went home, feeling like a failure.

Then she showed her husband the contract.

"Don't sign it. Compete," he advised.

Laura Lee's devastation turned into anger and then into action. She resigned. Within six days, she had a logo and a company name, LionShare Marketing, which reflected her determination. She also had her first client.

"I said to myself, I'm going to take the lion's share away from this guy," Laura Lee says. "I stood on the ledge, and I leapt into my own business."

Managing Her Worries

Her leap into entrepreneurism was a success. She was thirty-three years old when she started her company. Her business, which offered integrated marketing, consistently experienced double-digit growth and she micromanaged every aspect.

In 2006, Laura Lee's eleven-year-old Lenexa, Kansas, based company was expanding rapidly. She had thirteen employees and had recently bought a building and invested in a new product line. But despite her success, angst and worry kept her awake at night. She worked constantly and was consumed with guilt because she never had enough time with her husband and young daughter. She needed a place to unload her worries. She needed someone to guide and coach her.

Three years earlier, a friend had suggested that Laura Lee apply to HEMP. Instead, Laura Lee tried other business organizations, searching for a group of peers. But she couldn't find business owners that matched her own motivation and drive.

In 2006, Laura Lee's friend reminded her about HEMP.

"They grow you so you can grow your company," the friend said. "They help you change your behavior."

Leading from the Ledge

Laura Lee had always been a leader. At age five, she masterminded a backyard circus, bringing together all the neighborhood children and their dogs. Her parents had taught her tenacity, confidence, and perseverance. They said, "You can do anything you want. Just make sure you're happy." They cheered her on and offered suggestions for improvement.

Happily, Laura Lee rose to the top in her high school and college activities, serving as captain of the cheerleaders, the gymnastics team, and the track team.

"I didn't like waiting around for others to make decisions," Laura Lee says. "I wanted to get things done."

Laura Lee Meets Her Mentoring Match

Laura Lee entered HEMP in the fall of 2006. Her first meeting with her mentor, Ken Rashid, consultant, the KR Company, was memorable.

Laura Lee was complaining about the impossibility of balancing her life between her work demands and her need to spend time with her family.

"I feel so guilty because I can't pick up my daughter after school," she told him. Ken put up his hand to silence her.

"I don't want to hear another word about this," he said. "If you want to pick up your daughter after school, change your schedule. You own the business."

At first, Laura Lee thought, "How can he talk to me that way!"

Then, she felt relieved.

Ken Rashid,
consultant,
the KR Company

"His words were so empowering," she says. "It really was that simple. Change your mind and change your life."

She began picking up her daughter every Friday, a ritual that the two of them still enjoy.

Building up the A-Team

Ken helped her manage her workaholic tendencies.

"He helped me understand my top-performing behaviors and helped me define what I needed to do every day to be successful," Laura Lee says.

He also helped her hone her communications style.

Honesty was vital to Laura Lee. Ken showed her how to communicate truthfully in a more business-like way.

"It was all in the delivery," Laura Lee says. "I learned to tone myself down."

Instead of simply saying, "You are underperforming," Laura Lee learned to start with an apology. "I am so sorry that I have not done a good job of explaining this task to you. I want to make sure we are clear on what your responsibilities are. I'm going to be clearer going forward."

Ken also helped her plan for the further growth of her business.

She didn't have team leaders. She didn't have employees who could help take her to the next level. Ken urged her to let go of staff members who were not performing and put together an A-team.

"You can't move all the dirt yourself," he said. "You need a strategic team and you need employees who can take on some of the weight."

She also needed money to grow.

Upon the advice of other HEMPers, she went to a new bank and established a line of credit before she needed it.

Grounding the Organizational Tree

On a typical pre-HEMP day, any employee could walk into Laura Lee's office and consult her about any issue at any time. Her mentor helped her set boundaries. He taught her to say, "No."

"I'm always striving," Laura Lee says. "But that gets in the way of my family time. Ken encouraged me to do the best I can and then be done for the day."

With Ken's help, she created an organizational tree, with herself at the bottom, symbolizing her role as the foundation and root of the company. Ken worked with Laura Lee to identify the leaders in her company. They divided her staff into teams with each team having a manager. He met with those leaders monthly, helping them build their management skills.

"Don't let Laura Lee micromanage you," he told them.

It took the employees a while to adjust to the concept of team leaders.

"They still had access to me, but they couldn't just stroll in without an appointment," Laura Lee says. "They had to first go through their team leader."

Having team leaders helped the company in these ways:

- The team leaders made LionShare look larger to the outside world.

- The additional structure helped attract clients, letting her clients know she was big enough to handle new jobs.
- Employees felt more empowered. They did not have to wait to share ideas and concerns with Laura Lee; they now had team leaders to consult.
- With the team leaders, Laura Lee could concentrate on what she did best: sell.
- Her stress lessened as she realized she could count on the leaders: she did not have to keep checking in and monitoring.

"Instead of pouring my energy all over the place, I focused on what I'm good at, what I like, and what I have to do first," Laura Lee says. "I also became a better delegator."

Along with her focus, her ability to analyze the big picture blossomed.

"A world of options opened up," Laura Lee says. "I looked at my business in a much wider way. I asked myself questions, such as 'What do I do if I grow the business? How do I value the company? What if I wanted to merge, or sell?' In the past, I had never had such thoughts."

Peer Pleasure

Not only did Laura Lee have the coach she had been yearning for, but she also found a like-minded group of business owners.

"Going to a HEMP gathering reminded me I was not alone," Laura Lee says. "That was so eye-opening! To be able to walk up to another woman and say, 'Oh my God, my debt is now over $500,000. How will I ever pay it back?' and get guidance and support was phenomenal. HEMP was the gateway to all these amazing entrepreneurs."

Laura Lee Jones, Christina Friederichs, and Michelle Robin vote in another exciting new participant.

Growing Into the Job

Today, Laura Lee is focused on sales, with her team leaders supporting customer service. She has an in-house accountant and she's farming out her data work. Her staff has grown from thirteen in 2006 to twenty-five in 2011.

"We now have better reporting and financials," she says. "We have core measurements and reports. We know how many times we presented to a client and how many times we got the job."

"I am definitely clearer on my goals, whether personal or work-related," she says. "I am a kinder person with more patience and I have learned how to manage my time better."

She is also engaging in more broad-based thinking: analyzing how to strategically partner with companies and how to build sales teams.

Laura Lee has grown as a person, entrepreneur, and leader. Her company and staff have grown with her.

The Replay

THE SITUATION:

Laura Lee Jones was drowning in worry and overwork.
- She was trying to manage all the details of her business.
- She worked constantly and felt guilty that she didn't have enough time with her husband and daughter.

THE SOLUTION:

Grow yourself and grow your business.
- Concentrate on what you do best. Build teams to support you and avoid micromanaging.
- Know when to stop working and go home.

THE RESULTS:

Laura Lee is now connected with her family and is happier and more effective at work.
- Her business continues double-digit growth.
- Staff is at twenty-five employees, including three team leaders.
- She focuses on her strengths and looks at the big picture.

Joe Lieberman
and SPIDERtel:
**UNTANGLING AN
ACQUISITION**

"Ray Pitman doesn't email or text. How will I communicate with him?" Joe Lieberman asked.

That was Joe's first response in the fall of 2007, when he learned that Ray Pitman, founder, Pitman Manufacturing and RO Corporation, was slated to be his HEMP mentor. Joe knew Ray was highly regarded and had a wealth of entrepreneurial experience. But Joe was CEO of SPIDERtel, a web development business. He couldn't imagine learning from a guy who didn't have a clue about computers.

Still, Joe decided to give Ray a try.

Ray Pitman,
founder,
Pitman Manufacturing,
RO Corporation

"That was one of the best decisions I ever made," Joe says.

They talked on the phone and met in person. Joe quickly learned that mentoring had little to do with technical knowledge of the industry and more to do with business fundamentals, human relationships, and cash management.

Wanting Adult Supervision

In early 2007, SPIDERtel was doing well but had reached a plateau in terms of growth.

"I was interested in getting 'adult supervision,'" says Joe, who was then forty-three years old. "I needed someone who could give me advice."

Joe had grown into his entrepreneurial spirit gradually. After getting an engineering degree from the University of Michigan in 1986, he realized one thing: "I did not want to be an engineer."

He soon signed on with Sprint, working in business development. But when offered a chance to become president of a start-up business focused on tele-communications and pay phone management, he took it.

"Once I got the taste of running a business, I became 'unemployable,'" Joe jokes.

During that time period, he earned an MBA in management and marketing at the University of Missouri-Kansas City. When cell phones decimated the pay phone industry, his current business died and Joe began selling web services on his own. In 1996, he started SPIDERtel, which grew organically, one client and one employee at a time. In 2007, Joe had thirteen employees and more than a million dollars in annual revenue.

Unweaving the Tangled Web

When he applied to HEMP in early 2007, Joe was interested in expanding and growing his business. But by the time Joe was assigned a mentor that fall, his priorities had changed: he was focused on salvaging his business.

Two years earlier, SPIDERtel had acquired a small web development business. Joe had a good working relationship with the two people who ran the business and had counted on one of them to help the new portion of the company advance technologically.

But that didn't happen.

Quality control went down and SPIDERtel began losing clients. As a result of the business acquisition, Joe had taken on some accounts that possessed great potential. But those acquired accounts were draining away his new resources and their payoff seemed questionable.

"It was a double whammy," Joe says. "I couldn't generate revenue from those accounts, but I was spending time and resources trying to fulfill them."

He asked HEMP for help and they put together a SWOT (Strengths Weaknesses Opportunities Threats) team of a half-dozen people.

"We met in my conference room and I spilled my guts," Joe says. "Then we identified the problems and the solutions."

Part of the problem, Joe learned, was his tolerance of poor performance from his employees.

"I wasn't taking strong action to triage the situation," he says. "I had suspected that was an issue and this meeting was a validation. It was also humbling, scary, and a relief."

Joe had hard decisions to make. If he terminated one of his two new employees, he worried both would leave and he'd be in a mess, since these employees were key architects in several of his new strategies. But Ray and his SWOT team urged him to staunch the bleeding. It took him six months to find a replacement for one employee and another six months to replace the other.

During this difficult period, Ray helped Joe assess his options. Joe went to his accounts and renegotiated payment terms so the business could survive. He let go of one large account that was sucking the business dry; he knew he couldn't finish the project in a timely basis.

"I lost a half-million dollars over that period," Joe says. "I would have lost a lot more if I hadn't freed up those resources."

During that time, Joe also did his best to change his own behavior.

"I had an unfounded optimism that I could fix things." Joe says. "I learned there can be a severe downside for giving people the benefit of the doubt for too long."

Even during those difficult years, Joe continued to do an excellent job of marketing his business and developing outstanding products. He built an award-winning company he was proud of. All along the way, he sought advice and adapted and kept the company going.

Still, when an opportunity came for him to sell SPIDERtel, he was ready for a change.

"I no longer loved what I was doing and I wanted to do work I was passionate about," he says.

Starting a Start-Up Again

By spring 2011, Joe was in a new health-care start-up, serving as president of BillMediator.com. The company works with hospitals to provide bill settlements for patients and providers.

He's learned from his previous experiences.

Mentees Elizabeth Amirahmadi and Joe Lieberman.

"My tolerance for poor performance is short," he says. "I value customer service more than I ever did and want to emulate the best business practices possible."

He also does consulting work, using his skills to essentially mentor his clients. Several of his clients are already experiencing noticeable improvements.

For Joe, his personal improvements continue.

"I am always open to advice and learning," he says.

The Replay

THE SITUATION:

Joe Lieberman was worried he'd lose his business.

- Quality control was slipping.
- Expenses were mounting.
- His employees were not supporting him.

THE SOLUTION:

- Seek help and be open about discussing all the issues.
- Challenge your preconceived ideas.
- Know that you can't turn bad employees into good employees.
- Solve your problems quickly so you can focus on productive efforts.

THE RESULTS:

Joe's willingness to change his own behavior kept his business afloat.

- Joe replaced the difficult employees.
- He kept the business running during difficult times.
- Even during the challenging period, he provided excellent customer service and products.

Photo by Bruce Mathews.

Mary Lou Jacoby and Warehouse 1:

GETTING FOCUSED AND FINANCIALLY SOUND

Mary Lou Jacoby's initial business plan was simple: earn enough money to feed herself and her ten-year-old son. It was 1986 and she was in her mid-thirties, a single mom fresh out of a long-term relationship. She had been an integral part of her boyfriend's family business. When the relationship ended, she lost her job and her house.

"I was starting over," she says.

Mary Lou had no college degree. But she was resilient, and she loved new ideas and change. She had experience in the scrap metal and junk business. She knew how to buy, and she hated to see anything of value going to waste. She started wandering around Kansas City, buying used office furniture and equipment from big corporations and selling it to start-ups. She had no business model and no plan, beyond survival.

Her concept was successful. In 1988, she incorporated as Warehouse 1. In 1998, Warehouse 1 was named one of the Kansas City Chamber's top ten small businesses.

"I had a growing business that I wanted to make bigger and better," Mary Lou says. "But I didn't know how."

Help from HEMP

Help came in the form of an invitation to participate in HEMP.

In 2000, when Mary Lou joined HEMP, she had thirty employees and sales of more than $5 million. Her goal was to learn how to grow the business and make it a success for the people involved.

Bill Eddy,
dean emeritus,
UMKC Bloch School
of Business

Initially, her awe of her mentor, Bill Eddy, dean emeritus of the UMKC Bloch School of Business, nearly held her back.

"At first, I didn't know how to benefit from the mentoring process," she says. "I was too scared to ask for help."

Everyone in the HEMP group was so willing to help that she soon became less intimidated and more comfortable.

"HEMP was like a smorgasbord, a talent pool of some of the smartest business people in the Midwest," she says. "I realized if I didn't ask for assistance, they wouldn't know how to help me."

Embracing Change and Fueling Growth and Leadership

Mary Lou reached out for accounting, operations, and human relations help.

"I didn't know how important cost accounting was," she says. "I was operating with no product costs; I lumped my entire inventory together. That meant my financial statements were of no value. I only knew the bank account was growing."

She was ready to ask tough questions, such as: "What are we doing that makes money? What should we be doing more of and what should we quit doing?"

The answers led her to change the entire accounting system. She instituted cost accounting and a new inventory system, so she could see what was profitable and what wasn't.

"Over time, I changed every facet of the business, including what we bought, the direction of our marketing, the customer base, our vendors, and our delivery method," she says. "We are open to ongoing change and review our systems every month as part of our financials."

Going through such a process required Mary Lou to become a better and more effective leader.

"I had to quit being so involved in the daily grind and to trust my colleagues and associates," she says.

At some point, she decided she wanted her associates to be the most sought after people in the industry, so she gave them more responsibility.

"We developed a good internal training program, offering seminars and tuition assistance," Mary Lou says. "We encouraged people to increase their value to the company and to society."

Mentoring Made a Difference

One of her key turning points was becoming a vendor for the federal government. She worked for three years to get the contracts.

"It was a time-consuming process but I wasn't going to give up because I knew we could do it," Mary Lou says. Her determination and persistence paid off. Today, government contracts are a steady part of her revenue stream.

Graduating from HEMP was another turning point. She was pleased when HEMP invited her to become a mentor.

"Every time I meet with my mentees, I learn something," she says.

For Mary Lou, her mentors have made a crucial difference in her business's success.

"Get a mentor if you don't have one," she advises. "Pick someone you can meet with and talk to. There's someone in your industry, a vendor, a customer, that you can go to and say, 'Can we have lunch?'"

Today, Warehouse 1 is an international company with fifty employees and yearly sales of more than $10 million. Mary Lou and her associates are still growing and changing, always striving to discover their best.

Mary Lou Jacoby displaying her wonderful sense of humor.

The Replay

THE SITUATION:

Mary Lou Jacoby had a successful business and wanted to make it bigger and better.

- Her accounting system was not effective.
- Her financial statements weren't useful.
- Her employee training was minimal.
- Her business operations needed analysis and revision.

THE SOLUTION:

- Seek and listen to advice from mentors and peers.
- Re-evaluate every aspect of the company.
- Set up an ongoing financial review process.
- Develop an internal training program and empower the employees.

THE RESULTS:

Mary Lou builds a dynamic and growing international business.

- Her revenues are greater than $10 million.
- Her staff grew to fifty employees.
- She and her company are reaching out into the community to offer mentoring assistance.

6

REFUSING
TO GIVE UP

Gary Short and Sys-Tek:

BUILDING CONFIDENCE AND
REBUILDING BUSINESS

Photo by Bruce Mathews.

"I was five minutes from going out of business," says Gary Short, president, Sys-Tek Companies, in Blue Springs, Missouri.

It was 2005 and Gary's ten-year-old mechanical and electrical engineering consulting firm was in serious trouble. Gary, age forty-eight, had depended primarily on tele-communications customers. Then the telecom industry tanked. Gary had also opened up a Texas office without first researching its potential. That decision further strained cash and resources. The company's revenues plummeted from $3.2 million to half a million. Key employees left, and Gary's work force, once twenty-eight strong, dwindled to two. Customers lost confidence in the firm. Worst of all, Gary lost confidence in himself.

When an employee suggested he apply for HEMP, Gary dispiritedly filled out the application, certain that his business was such a shambles he wouldn't be accepted.

"HEMP called and made an appointment to come see me," he says. "I figured they would be here for ten minutes, then throw up their hands and leave."

Gary was honest with the HEMP team, revealing the company's precarious status. When they accepted him into the mentoring program, he was surprised and grateful.

An Entrepreneur Is Born

Gary had never had a mentor. He had never really had a father. He grew up poor in Kansas City's urban core and dreamed of running his own business.

"I wanted to better my circumstances," Gary says. "I figured being my own boss would be a step forward, but I didn't know how to get started."

As he was growing up, no one advised him. No one mentioned college. He graduated from high school and went to work in a shoe store. In 1976, at age nineteen, Gary was already a father.

"I was determined my son would have the opportunities I didn't get," he says.

But how? Gary didn't know what to do. A friend asked, "What subjects did you like in school?"

"Math and science were easy for me," Gary said.

"Why don't you look into engineering?"

"What has math got to do with driving a train?" Gary asked.

Gary soon learned about the different kinds of engineers. He bought textbooks for all the courses he hadn't yet taken, read voraciously, audited classes, studied hard and took the engineering certification test and passed.

"I fell in love with mechanical and electrical engineering," he says. "I knew I would start my own company. I just didn't know when."

For years, he worked hard for others. From 1988 to 1994, he owned 33 percent interest in an engineering firm.

"That was a great education," Gary says. "We grew from six to fifty people. We split up due to a clash of egos."

In 1995, when the eighteen-month noncompete period ended, Gary created an office in his basement and started Sys-Tek.

In the beginning, the going was so easy, Gary thought, "Why doesn't everyone have a company like this?" He was an established engineer and knew how to develop clients and create proposals. Money and customers flowed in. As sole owner and president, Gary managed it all, until the ten-year point. Then the market dried up and the employees bailed out. His cash was short, and his mood grew dark.

"I was still in business only because I wasn't good at accounting," Gary says. "I didn't know I was broke."

Monday Mornings with Ray

On December 1, 2005, mentor Ray Pitman arrived at Sys-Tek. Ray was retired from a career in the construction industry. He had experienced his share of business successes and failures.

The mentoring process started with a lot of honest conversation.

"Ray and I talked about everything," Gary says. Ray wanted to learn about Gary Short. He listened to Gary's personal and business history and he talked to Gary's wife and sons.

"My work with Ray became a family affair," Gary says. "Ray was the father I never had."

Ray told Gary, "This company is still alive as long as you continue to work at it."

For the first time in his life, Gary had a coach and a cheerleader.

"As a business owner, you rarely have anyone patting you on the back," Gary says. "My confidence was destroyed and Ray gradually built it back up."

They met every Monday morning for three years. During those sessions they analyzed what was going right and what needed fixing. They talked about financials, families, feelings, and the future. Gary took Ray with him to client interviews.

"My clients had seen many of my employees leave and wondered if I could hang in there," Gary says. "Meeting Ray boosted their faith in me."

Ray helped Gary look at the big picture. He reviewed the organizational chart, noticing how involved Gary was in all the business details. Ray asked, "How can the business evolve so the president isn't wearing every hat?"

Ray Pitman,
founder,
Pitman Manufacturing,
RO Corporation

Marking the Milestones

Six months into the program, Gary regained his confidence and also took responsibility for some of the problems his decision-making had caused.

"Ray's pointed questions and honest communication allowed me to look at the company from the inside out," Gary says. "Employees had told me what I wanted to hear. Ray told me the truth."

Gary had been managing his company's engineering division and its commissioning ("MAKE-IT-WORK") division. With Ray's encouragement, Gary created a director's position for each division.

"Bringing in those key people was a huge change," Gary says. "It was hard for me to give up the control, but I realized I couldn't continue as before."

Ray also encouraged Gary to make sure he had access to cash.

Together they approached banks for a line of credit. Bank after bank turned Gary down. They persisted until they found a bank willing to extend the credit and develop a relationship.

But they didn't stop there. Ray wanted Sys-Tek to have a back-up plan, so Gary developed working relationships with two banks.

By the third year of the program, all the ideas, flexible thinking and hard work started to come together. Sys-Tek had a strong new foundation and Gary had a renewed sense of confidence and an increased passion for his business.

The HEMP Legacy Continues

Today, Gary is still involved with HEMP as a graduate of the program and is a major contributor. He has made smart business decisions and the business has grown so significantly that he has had serious acquisition offers. Here are some of Gary's key learnings from Ray and the program:

Always Have a Plan B

"Ray advised me to problem-solve for the future," Gary says. "That was new thinking for me. If I'd been more future-oriented, I could have prevented the company pitfalls."

Ray encouraged Gary to learn more about his own financial statements. Through HEMP training, Gary learned to forecast his financial needs.

Find the Pearls among Your Peers

Gary found a wealth of help through discussions with other HEMP participants and graduates.

"Hearing about other people's struggles helped me put my problems in perspective," Gary says. "It was also useful to discuss common issues, such as health insurance, taxes, and employee challenges."

The HEMP group has a high level of confidentiality and a deep loyalty.

"I know I can always call someone in the group and get help," Gary says. "It's better than Googling. We're a uniquely connected community."

Gary and Teresa Short enjoying Celebrate HEMP luau.

THE SITUATION:

Gary Short had lost clients, status, employees, money, and worst of all, confidence.

- His customer base eroded, due to reliance on one industry and market downturn.
- Staff was decimated; employees dwindled from twenty-eight to two.
- Revenues plummeted, down from $3.2 million to half a million.

THE SOLUTION:

- Know you can do it. If you keep coming to work, the business has a chance.
- Understand your financial statements and build relationships with banks.
- Go beyond the details and create a strategic plan.

THE RESULTS:

Gary builds an exceptional business that serves his clients and feeds his soul.

- Revenues climbed back to $2.7 million.
- Staff is at eighteen employees, including a director for each division.
- The client base is diversified.
- The business has a healthy credit line.

Photo by Bruce Mathews.

Dan McDougal and Dredge America:
DREDGING UP GOOD COMMUNICATIONS AND HUMAN RELATIONS

It was fall 2000, and nothing was going right for Dan McDougal. Over the last ten years, his company, Dredge America, had been rich and poor three times. But now, the company seemed on the brink of going under. It was several months behind paying vendors. Dan juggled a dozen credit cards to create a trickle of cash. He'd sold everything he could sell and maxed out his bank credit line.

"Making money wasn't the problem," Dan says. "Keeping a flow of money and growing the business was the problem. I wanted advice from people with more experience and education."

From Furniture-making to Building Bridges to Dredging

Earlier in his career, Dan had been so confident of his abilities he didn't feel the need for much advice.

He began his entrepreneurial journey in high school, when he built furniture and sold it out of his garage. He managed real estate and did painting and carpentry while he put himself through engineering school at what was then the University of Missouri-Rolla. One night, he was sitting on the porch of his apartment building and he overheard people from a local sign company giving the bookstore next door a bid to create and install a sign.

"I heard how high the price was, and I thought, I can make a sign," Dan says.

He recruited an artist friend, ordered some lettering, and started a company. When he heard of someone needing a sign, he offered a conceptual design and a price.

"Rather than settling for a nine-to-five job, I offered to fix someone else's problem, determining my own price," Dan says. "That way, I had no boundaries, and I could get compensated for my creativity."

Once he graduated, he wanted to broaden his engineering experience, so he went to work for a large bridge contractor: first as an estimator, then engineer, then manager. By age twenty-six, he was managing a $33 million bridge project with seventy-five employees. Three years later, when he had completed the project, his employer offered him a territory in Wisconsin. But Dan didn't want to move north.

"Instead I decided to start my own company," he says.

In 1990, he formed McDougal Construction, working out of an old barn in Kansas City, Missouri, and began building and repairing bridges and constructing dams. His former employer was his first client.

The company was doing well and in 1994, Dan bought a small local dredging company. A year later, Dan sold the bridge division, changed the company name to Dredge America, and began offering professional hydraulic dredging services on a national level. Using specialized equipment, Dredge America dredged channels, marinas, golf courses, mines, power plants, and more.

"I did well for several years," Dan says. "I thought I had the golden touch and could make money anywhere."

Learning the Hard Way

But his magic touch turned to fool's gold. He spent a million dollars on new equipment and opened a sand-and-gravel mining operation in Dallas.

"I did my research and nine out of ten of my assumptions were correct," Dan says. The tenth detail was his downfall: The material his company mined was too fine for commercial use. Most of what had been dredged up sifted back in the pit.

"Today I would tell any mentee to test the waters first and lease the equipment," Dan says. "But I was too smart to need advice back then."

The new business opened in January and closed in December. In the process, six years of hard work and most of his net worth went down the drain.

Dan cut his losses and moved on, slowly rebuilding the company. Then he bid on two projects. The first was an innovative wetland protection enterprise, using the dredges to fill more than two miles of geotubes along the back side of Galveston Island in Texas. The filled geotubes resembled large sausages and stuck out of the shallow water to block the waves.

"The geotubes were fairly new technology. The project ended up taking about three times the labor and twice the equipment we estimated," Dan says. "So we were pretty financially wiped out and back where we started...again."

But he had already committed to another geotube job along the Gulf Coast with the Army Corps of Engineers, placing six hundred feet of the tubes on top of a rock jetty. His company bid on the venture during storm season, and could not inspect the top of the jetty, which was under water. They had assumed the jetty had a level surface as shown on the plans, but once work began, they quickly learned it was very uneven and covered with sharp barnacles.

"We tried to tell the Corps that the waves would rip away the tubes," Dan said. "But they insisted we continue. We had posted a bond and had no choice."

The crew could only work during calm sea days. They were on standby for eight months just to complete what should have been two weeks of actual construction work. Within a week, the waves destroyed the tubes, just as Dan predicted. Dredge America filed a claim, trying to get back some of the hundreds of thousands of dollars the company had poured into the project. Meanwhile, Dan was distracted by the emotional and financial toll of the lawsuit, and the company floundered. After years of exhausting legal wrangling, they settled for 10 percent of the claim.

"Sometimes life is not fair," Dan says. "But the cost of proving you are right is higher than you can afford."

Getting Through the Crisis and Starting to Refocus

Dan was at his lowest when he joined HEMP in 2000.

His mentor, Ray Pitman, assured him, "I have been in worse shape, and I survived."

Those words inspired Dan to push through the difficulties and come up with solutions.

One of the first things Ray helped Dan improve was his communication style. As an engineer, Dan was efficient and direct. His emailed memos gave people facts, instructions, and directions.

"Some employees find your memos offensive and unappreciative," Ray told him.

No one had ever given Dan such feedback.

"Ray's comments transformed my communication style," Dan says. "If I had something positive to say, I sent it in writing. If it was negative, I talked to the employee."

Ray also shared his own personal business experiences, both good and bad. This made the mentoring experience much more real and effective. Dan realized that he was not the only business owner who had made mistakes. Hearing personal stories of how others had survived and prevailed under similar or worse circumstances provided the inspiration to keep moving forward, despite the odds.

Ray Pitman,
founder,
Pitman Manufacturing,
RO Corporation

Turning Over and Turning Around

Turnover was another huge issue for the company. Dan did the hiring, and he was not adept at the process.

"I'd talk to a person for five minutes and hire him," he recalls. "No background check.

No reference review. No detailed description of what the job really entailed."

As part of the mentoring connection, Ray got to know Dan's wife, Renee. He noticed her human relations skills and felt she would be an asset to the company. But the McDougals believed couples should not work together. They worried that it would damage their relationship.

Ray thought differently.

"He convinced us that Renee should work in human resources," Dan says. "Her skills, her professionalism, and her ability to read people made a dramatic difference in our business."

Ray also believed in hiring the smartest people for each position. Renee took his advice and transformed the hiring process, conducting extensive interviews and background and reference checks. The field employees worked three weeks out of town, then had one week off. She explained the job and the travel schedule. Over time, she replaced the employees who weren't working out and hired employees who thrived on the work and travel. Once the quality of the employees rose, turnover diminished.

Letting Go of Control

For Dan, stepping back from the hiring process was a personal growth experience.

"I finally realized that each company decision did not depend on me," he says. "That was difficult, because at some point I had performed every single position in the company."

Dan also realized his ability to perform many tasks fairly well was actually a curse, not a blessing, for his growing business. He needed to let other people take over some of the roles he had been filling and focus his own energies on big-picture thinking.

"As the founder, I had a hard time letting go," he says. "But I knew if the company was to grow, I couldn't do everything. I had to let go."

Once his company improved its hiring process, Dan went above and beyond to keep the employees. The company recognized employee birthdays and anniversaries with cards and gifts, performed annual career development reviews, housed the traveling employees in nice condos and vacation homes instead of motels, provided high-level professional training, matched IRA contributions, and honored each employee's contribution to the business.

Mentee Renee McDougal with mentor Ray Pitman enjoy the Fresh Air Farm shindig.

"We have incredible employees now," Dan says. "There was definitely a direct relationship between getting the right people and making our company a financial success."

Today, the company is thriving, and so is the McDougals' relationship. They have checks and balances in place, so they can limit their liability and expenses on individual projects. They intend to create a management team that will eventually replace them both. They are grooming one person for operations, one for business development and one for finance and accounting.

"Over a period of a few years, we had created an entirely new and different culture," Dan says.

The HEMP team and Dan's willingness to learn and change have been key components in the growth of his company.

"I am a life-long student," he says. "I believe I can learn from anyone, anywhere, and I do that constantly."

The Replay

THE SITUATION:

Dan McDougal struggled with unstable cash flow and high employee turnover.
- Casual hiring practices and poor communication triggered employee turnover.
- Overspending on equipment drained the company's resources.

THE SOLUTION:

- Communicate in a less terse, more personal manner with the employees.
- Put positive feedback in writing. For negative feedback, talk directly to the employee.
- Implement professional hiring practices.
- Go all out to get the best people; then go above and beyond to keep them.
- Be willing to learn from your own mistakes.

THE RESULTS:

Dan reduces turnover, builds an exceptional team of employees and institutes checks and balances.
- Revenues and growth are steady and climbing.
- Turnover is diminished.
- The right people are in the right positions.

Laura Laiben and the Culinary Center of Kansas City:
COOKING UP CREATIVE BUSINESS SOLUTIONS

"You have to choose," the doctor said sternly. "You must be on complete bed rest. You can either have a job or a baby but you can't have both."

It was 1989 and thirty-one-year-old Laura Laiben was two months pregnant with her first child. Prior to her pregnancy, her job had been her life. She had practiced tax and securities law with a prestigious Kansas City law firm, then moved up to working in public finance and bonds. She was working on a multimillion-dollar bond deal when the doctor gave her the ultimatum.

She chose her child.

Finding the Recipe for Happiness

For seven months, she was bed-bound. The partners at her law firm were not happy; they didn't seem to understand that the situation was out of her control.

"I did a lot of meditation and soul searching," she says. "During this time, I realized that I didn't want to continue working as a lawyer. I asked myself, 'How can you fashion the life you want?' In order to do that, I had to figure out what made me happy."

When she conjured up happy memories, she thought of the feeling of connection she experienced sitting on her grandmother's kitchen counter as a little girl, making pie dough.

"My whole family enjoyed cooking," she says. "As a child, I made every recipe in *Betty Crocker's New Boys and Girls Cookbook*. Some of the most wonderful things in my life happened around a table and I wanted to share those experiences with others."

Over the months of her confinement, she began designing her new business. She saw a niche for teaching the home cook without the restrictions of an accredited program. She also had a strong desire to create a work environment that fostered each employee's natural strengths and provided ways for employees to keep their lives in balance.

Once her child was born, she did some part-time legal work and began looking at property. It took her several years to refine her concept and find the right location.

"In 1996, five years after the birth of my second child, I found a building in downtown Overland Park, Kansas, and I jumped off the edge," she says.

The Culinary Center of Kansas City debuted in 1998, offering cooking classes and private events, including a corporate team-building program.

In July 1998, before Laura had even technically opened, the food editor of the *Kansas City Star* wrote an article about the center and three hundred phone calls flooded Laura's office.

She had created a unique business concept and people were eager to participate.

Mike O'Malley,
president,
O'Keeffe & O'Malley,
Inc.

Learning the Ingredients of Small Business Success

In 2003, the HEMP team invited Laura to join the program.

She began working with her mentor Mike O'Malley, president of O'Keeffe & O'Malley, Inc., and other HEMP members and attended HEMP events, enjoying the sense of support and community. Though her law degree was useful, she had much to learn about running a small business. A year into the program Mike moved to Denver and Grant Burcham, president and CEO, Missouri Bank, became Laura's new mentor. She was so impressed with his business philosophy, knowledge, and kindness that she moved her accounts over to his bank.

Grant Burcham,
president and CEO,
Missouri Bank

From the Cooking Class into the Fire

Two years into Laura's HEMP experience, an employee rushed into her office and said, "You might want to grab your purses and get out. There's a fire next door."

Laura grabbed her purse and got everyone safely out of her building. Then she watched as smoke invaded her business and firemen poured two million gallons of water into the space next door.

When it was safe to go inside once again, Laura was devastated by the extensive smoke and water damage. Within hours, she began receiving calls from HEMPers wanting to help. She gratefully accepted the support. Her business was in a precarious position, since she would have to close for clean up and she still had to meet payroll and other expenses.

But she was prepared for emergencies.

"Please move the money from the reserve fund into our account," she told a trusted person who helped with the financial part of the business.

That's when she learned there was no reserve fund left; that person had squandered the money and run up considerable credit card and other debt. She was suddenly in an even more precarious position.

She turned to Grant for help. He suggested she come to the bank at once. There she was met with the paperwork for a line of credit, strategic advice, and personal support.

She squeaked through the crisis and for several years she concentrated on untangling her personal life, taking care of her children, and helping her company survive.

"An entrepreneur doesn't just have to deal with the business," Laura says. "The entrepreneur's whole life has to fit together."

Her bonds with other HEMPers helped her get through the adversity.

Happy times abound with Melody Warren, Laura Laiben, and Kay Julian.

"In those difficult years, everyone knew what was going on and everyone was very nice to me," she says. "People really meant it when they said, 'Call me if I can do anything for you.' I had to get beyond the fear of asking for help."

Full plates accompany Laura Laiben and Bill Eddy at another food-filled gathering.

Cooking up New Ideas

Through HEMP she had learned the concept of "putting your worst foot forward" and talking about failures and challenges. She also learned how fearless and flexible she was.

"Entrepreneurs have a different kind of cell in their bodies," she says. "We are not afraid of failing; we are only afraid of not trying. When we share things that we're not as proud of, that's when we open up and learn."

Laura kept trying. During those stressful years, the long-awaited opportunity to expand her physical space opened up. Midway through the expansion, she faced an additional challenge – an economic recession. Once again, her passion for her business and a big dose of perseverance helped her work through the tough times.

Because of the recession, she lost a significant source of revenue, since many of her corporate clients no longer had a budget for team building or private events.

"I had to get creative," she says.

So Laura started asking her clients, "What services can we provide for you?"

She learned that many companies still had a budget for community service and they still had the desire for team building. So she created a concept called All Hands for Hunger, which integrated team building and community service. Participants made food for specific charities, packaged it, wrote words of encouragement to the recipients, and delivered it. Then they sat down as a group and dined on what they created, while a facilitator provided feedback on how they worked together as a team.

A need for cash flow inspired another innovation: opening up her Tuesday staff lunch to the public. Customers often said, "Boy, you guys must eat well." Laura realized she could generate a little extra income and market her business and services if she offered a unique periodic staff lunch to the public. The program was a success and created a sense of community in the downtown area. After the customers left, Laura and her staff sat down to eat their own staff lunch together, enjoying a time of bonding and connection.

Creating Award-Winning Recipes for Success

When Laura started the business, she held about ten classes a month. Today, the Center hosts 550 cooking classes a year and more than 250 team building sessions and private events. Laura designed a retail space called Kitchenology and the center sells chef-prepared frozen dishes through its Dinners on Demand program.

To meet the country's insatiable appetite for barbeque, Laura created the Midwest BBQ Institute, which provides education in the art and science of smoking and grilling. Her current project is creating a wellness program for corporations, featuring healthy cooking for their employees.

"One of my job titles here is 'visionary,'" Laura says. "This title does not come with a crown but rather a responsibility to stay out of the details and make sure we're on course."

She's still involved with HEMP as a Fellow and served on the mentee committee for several years.

"You can't expect to travel through the journey of enterpreneurship without being impacted by circumstances beyond your control," she says. "I didn't expect a fire, a divorce, or a recession. But I've stayed agile and open to change and I've kept my passion for my business and my family and for doing work that makes me happy."

The Replay

THE SITUATION:
Laura Laiben experienced a devastating business and personal loss that imperiled her company.
- She had no emergency reserves.
- She had to keep her business afloat while making repairs and refurbishing.
- She had to deal with a tangle of personal issues.

THE SOLUTION:
- Ask for help.
- Ask your clients what they want and need.
- Use challenges to inspire creative thinking.

THE RESULTS:
Laura expands her services and continues to thrive in her business.
- Her company is voted one of the top ten places to work in Kansas City.
- She adds services that enhance her marketing niche.
- She leads by being flexible and creative and considering the business overview.

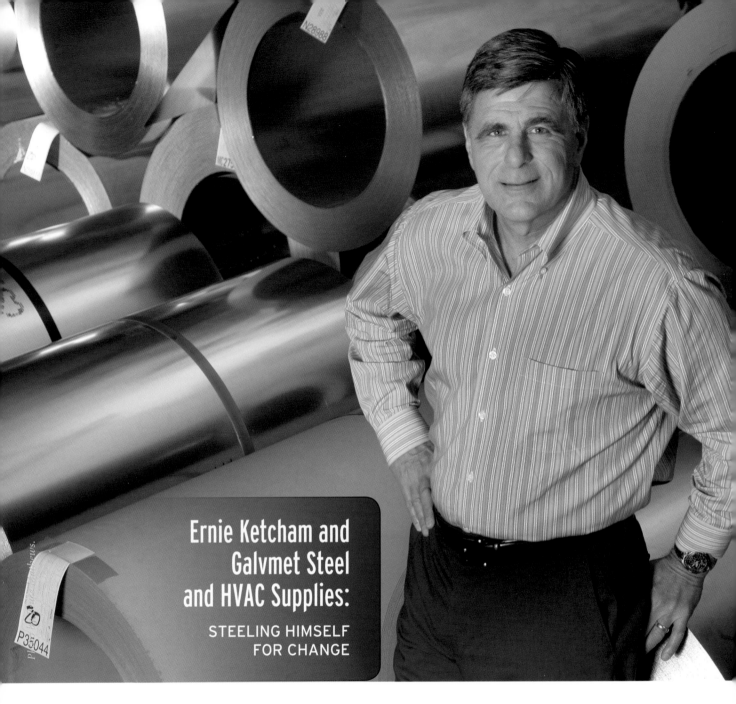

Ernie Ketcham and Galvmet Steel and HVAC Supplies:
STEELING HIMSELF FOR CHANGE

Ernie Ketcham, president/CEO of Galvmet Steel and HVAC Supplies, was a successful entrepreneur, with twenty-four employees, $14 million in revenue, and a yearly net profit of $1.5 million. When he joined HEMP in September of 2008, his goal was simple: to significantly grow his company.

A month later, Ernie's goal radically changed.

"I just wanted my business to survive," he says.

In October 2008, when the economy fell apart and the market plummeted, the price of steel rose to a historic high. Ernie's profit margin evaporated.

"We were instantly in a financially precarious situation," Ernie says. "We had to pour money into the company just to stay afloat."

His HEMP mentor, Dick Benner, project manager and board director of Executive Service Corp. of Greater Kansas City, rushed in to help. He and Ernie reviewed Galvmet's expenses and painstakingly cut $1 million out of his $3 million operating budget.

"We scrutinized all expenditures," Ernie says. "We canceled a phone card that cost $80 a month. We had been providing our employees with uniforms. We canceled the uniform service and issued T-shirts. We renegotiated our rent so we could pay only 50 percent for eight months. Every dollar mattered."

He also had to let go of seven employees.

"It was a stressful period," Ernie says. "Several times, I considered jumping off a bridge. But I'm a former Marine and failure was not an option."

Dick Benner,
retired corporate officer,
Avon Products

Building a Career of Steel

Ernie had worked in the steel business since 1977. He was transferred to Kansas City, Missouri, from Cleveland, Ohio, in 1990 to manage a branch of a large national service center. In February 1992, when Ernie learned that the company was going into Chapter 11 bankruptcy, he decided to start his own business.

"I knew the operational aspects of the business but didn't understand the financial side," he says. He asked a lot of people for advice and quickly put together a business plan. On April 30, his old company closed its doors. On May 5, Ernie opened the doors to Galvmet Steel.

His operational knowledge, his determination, and his intuitive business sense helped make Galvmet a success.

In 1994, he bought a leveler, a giant machine that flattened and cut coils of steel. Previously, his company had bought cut sheets of steel from another mill.

"The day the leveler arrived at my warehouse, our supplier experienced serious problems and shut down for a year," Ernie says. "We would have been out of business if I hadn't purchased that machine."

Having his own leveler reduced outside processing costs and gave him more flexibility on inventory. The leveler also made Galvmet more competitive and more profitable.

"We could cut exactly what we needed and we could offer our customers custom-cutting," Ernie explains.

Adding Products for Profits

Earlier, Ernie had put together an advisory board and consistently sought and listened to their suggestions. He considered ways to expand his business.

In 2007, Ernie added HVAC (Heating, Ventilating, Air Conditioning) supplies, as a way to spur growth. Several competitors had told him HVAC accounted for 60 percent of their business so he decided to give the products a try. But he was so busy he didn't take time to market the new offerings. Most of his customers didn't know he was carrying the items.

That changed when his steel revenues tanked. With Dick's help, the company began actively marketing Galvmet's HVAC products. Ernie tried approaches he had never used, such as direct mail and email campaigns. He offered weekly specials and trained his sales force to more aggressively market their new products.

"Initially, we were only selling galvanized sheets and coil and now we sell everything that comes out of the furnace," he says. "Some months HVAC revenues made the difference between profit and loss."

Asking for Help and Listening to Advice

"I'm disbanding the board, because I can no longer pay you," Ernie told his advisory team in 2009.

They all volunteered to stay on, without pay, and help Ernie through the tough period. The board urged him to restructure his payment terms with the large domestic steel mills, something Ernie had not considered.

"These mills represent our largest expense," Ernie says. "Every month, we spend $750,000 on coils of steel and we have to pay within thirty days."

Normally, the mills were inflexible on their payment terms. The board urged Ernie to be upfront with them, disclose his financial status, and ask for a respite in payment terms.

He followed their advice and went to his two major supplies. The mills allowed him a sixty-day payment window. Gradually, Ernie moved to a forty-five-day payment and then, when he regained financial stability, he returned to the usual thirty-day plan.

"Taking that action helped us get through that tough period and really solidified our relationship with one of the mills. We did everything as promised and they now really value us as a customer," Ernie says.

Recovering and Growing in Tough Times

"My chin is still above water," Ernie says.

He is grateful for his mentor, his advisers, and members of the HEMP community.

"These people gave me a shoulder to cry on," he says. "They propped me up and went beyond the role of advisers and mentors: they became friends."

Now, Ernie is trying to figure out how to move into another market, to offset the ongoing construction slump.

"Galvmet is good at distribution; maybe we can distribute a different product in a different industry," he says.

He hasn't yet figured out what that product is, but he knows he'll come up with the right solution. Of the last three years, Ernie says. "I knew I was resilient, but I'm much more resilient than I thought."

Dick Benner cuddles Kitty Ketcham while her husband, Ernie, watches the camera.

The Replay

THE SITUATION:

Ernie Ketcham was caught in a financial crisis when the economy fell and the construction industry faltered.

- Steel prices soared and Ernie's profit margin evaporated.
- He was desperate for ways to stay afloat during an economic downturn.

THE SOLUTION:

- Analyze all expenses and cut back wherever possible.
- Seek ideas from advisers and others.
- Look for new markets and revenue streams.
- Ask vendors to restructure payment plans.

THE RESULTS:

Ernie has successfully reduced expenses and built up his HVAC business.

- He's looking for other ways to diversify his revenue streams.
- He's tapped into his innate resilience and is determined to thrive in this difficult economic market.

UMKC LAW SCHOOL COURTROOM RENOVATION

Elizabeth Amirahmadi and International | Architects | Atelier:

ARCHITECT OF HER OWN COMPANY

Photo by Bruce Mathews.

Growing up in Mexico, Elizabeth Amirahmadi was brought up to go to college and then become a stay-at-home mom.

"When I started college, I never thought I would be working," she says.

Her family expected her to earn her degree and then get married. Initially she majored in accounting, but she found the subject boring. She was interested in home decorating. Her mother suggested she study something more practical–architecture.

With both parents' approval, Elizabeth moved from her home in Mazatlan to Guadalajara to study architecture. The work was hard and humbling; Elizabeth was used to being a top student and now she was struggling with the unfamiliar and complex concepts. In her third year of school, she signed up to be an exchange student in Nebraska.

"I signed up as a whim," she says. "I didn't even know where Nebraska was."

She was one of twelve students selected.

She continued her schooling and grew to love architecture. At college, she also met and married her husband. As they moved into the work force, she worked at small architectural firms. Her architect husband worked for a large firm. After some years, the couple began thinking, "If we were doing this project ourselves, we could give better service."

They'd been working for ten years and felt ready to start their own business. They figured all they needed was one good client. In 1988, the client came and Elizabeth and her husband began International | Architects | Atelier.

Beyond the Drawing Board

"When we thought of running our own company, we imagined designing and drawing," Elizabeth says. "Then reality hit and we realized we needed an office, employees, marketing, and more."

They had never experienced the administrative side of running a business. They had no management training and didn't know how to read financial statements.

"I just knew I had to keep the money coming in," she says.

Because they had young children, Elizabeth didn't want to travel. She concentrated on the administrative side of the business and her husband did the out-of-town project management.

As the company grew, so did the management issues and problems, particularly those that were personnel oriented.

"I felt dumb that I didn't know how to do business procedures," Elizabeth says. "I delayed firing people. Plus, I took things personally."

HEMP Instead of a Master's

In 2006, Elizabeth received an email inviting her to apply for HEMP.

"I was teaching a course at the university, running the business, and raising my kids," she says. "There was no way I could add in another commitment."

Meanwhile, the company's management issues persisted.

Elizabeth had no one to talk to about work and no female role models. She'd never experienced a mentor. All her family was in Mexico. Her friends were all architects and it didn't feel appropriate to discuss her problems with them. Her husband felt as lost as she did.

"My husband and I kept repeating the same business mistakes," she says. "I felt like I was hitting my head against the wall."

In 2007, when she received another invitation to join HEMP, she filled out the application.

Someone to Talk to and People to Listen to

Mentor Bob Shapiro, owner, Realty Consultants, instantly understood Elizabeth's staffing problems. She had hired a friend who'd worked loyally for years, but now wasn't doing her job. Other employees, also friends, weren't performing to their potential.

Bob Shapiro,
owner,
Realty Consultants

"You need to change your staffing," he advised.

Elizabeth knew he was right, but couldn't bring herself to take the action.

"But just having someone to discuss these issues with was incredible," she says.

Her mentor connected her with a HEMP program called Lunch with the Big Guy.

In that small group, led by Barnett Helzberg, each of the entrepreneurs talked about one of their pressing issues. She listened, realizing that everyone struggled with the same type of challenges.

"I had thought I was the only one with problems," she says.

At the luncheon, she discussed her staffing dilemma, focusing on her business manager.

"It's time to let her go," the other entrepreneurs advised. "You're going to be relieved when you fire her."

"It was affirming to hear other people echoing what I knew," she says. "I had doubted myself."

She walked out of the meeting feeling happy, supported, and ready to take action.

She let go of the employees who weren't working and hired new staff that supported the company's goals and mission.

"We now have a core of good people working with us," she says.

Learning from Other People's Mistakes

Elizabeth learned much from her HEMP classmates and from HEMP graduates and Fellows. When the economy spiraled downward, HEMP sponsored a panel of entrepreneurs who discussed how they had dealt with past setbacks.

Mentee Elizabeth Amirahmadi with her mentor, Bob Shapiro, celebrating her HEMP graduation.

One woman talked about a pivotal savings account. Her banker had suggested she put 3 percent of her income into savings.

"I never touch that money," the woman said.

Elizabeth thought the practice was a little strange, but decided to do it. She began saving 3 percent of all they received.

Elizabeth had a line of credit she'd used for years. When she needed additional cash flow, she simply called her bank and transferred money from her credit line.

One day, she called to transfer money to her checking account so she could meet the payroll.

"That money isn't available," the banker said.

"Why?" Elizabeth asked, her panic rising.

"The credit line is based on your accounts receivable. Your receivables aren't high enough, so your credit line didn't renew."

Elizabeth had a payroll due in two days. She paced her office, wracking her brain for options. Then she remembered her savings account.

"That account saved me," she says. "Without it, I wouldn't have been able to make payroll."

The savings account still stands in reserve.

Building a Stronger Business

Participating in HEMP has positively changed Elizabeth's business, her management style, and her outlook. Through the mentoring and the HEMP community, Elizabeth has gained more confidence in her own business acumen. From being around entrepreneurs who are direct communicators, she's been able to more easily express herself and articulate her likes and dislikes. She tries to resolve issues early on before they become problems. She also doesn't take business problems so personally.

"I'm more able to appreciate what I accomplish," she says. "I'm more comfortable sharing my ideas and that makes me a stronger business partner."

Though her business struggled during the tough economic times, she didn't lay off any employees.

"HEMP gave me the courage to move through the challenges," she says. "It helps to know you're not alone."

The Replay

THE SITUATION:

Elizabeth Amirahmadi kept repeating the same management and personnel mistakes.

- She had flagging confidence.
- She lacked management and financial experience.
- Her friends she hired years ago were lagging in job skills.
- She didn't have the skills or confidence to change the situation.
- She didn't have anyone to discuss and problem solve with.
- She took these business problems personally, blaming and doubting herself.

THE SOLUTION:

- Know that others struggle with similar issues.
- Separate emotions from the problems.
- Learn from mentors and HEMPers.
- Strengthen decision-making skills.

THE RESULTS:

Elizabeth built a core team of strong, dedicated employees and became a more skilled and confident leader.

- Business has a back-up savings account.
- The business moved through difficult economic times with its staff intact.
- Elizabeth has expanded her perspective and strengthened her management skills.
- She's looking at the big picture and analyzing business options and opportunities.

Missy Love and Alaskan Fur:
FASHIONING FINANCIAL SAVVY

Photo by Bruce Mathews.

"My mentor is not working out," Missy Smart, president of Alaskan Fur Company, told the HEMP director during the spring of 2002. "We're not communicating well."

The director knew that Bill Love, managing member of W.P. Love, was an excellent mentor. He was a successful and creative entrepreneur. His background in finance, venture capital, and private equity made him a good match for Missy and her company.

"Why don't you stick with it a little longer?" the director suggested. "I'll call Bill and talk to him."

Missy agreed to give Bill Love another try.

From Advertising to Operations

Missy Smart grew up in her family's business, a nationally known furrier that manufactures and sells fur and leather products. As a young teenager, she answered phones, gift wrapped packages, and helped in the office. She earned a degree in journalism from the University of Kansas. After graduation in 1984, she landed a marketing position in a local Kansas City company. While she was waiting for the job to start, her father asked her to help with some advertising decisions. Her assistance soon grew into a full-time job. For years she ran the marketing and advertising for Alaskan Fur. In the early 1990s, she became president and began running the entire operation. The transition felt natural.

"I've always liked fashion and it was interesting to be involved in the buying and manufacturing of products," Missy says. "I knew a lot about the industry from being around the business all my life."

Missy wanted to diversify and grow the company. But that wasn't always easy in a successful well-established family business. She saw the possibilities for expansion and she also understood her area of weakness: financials.

"Forecasting, planning, budgeting, and reading financial statements weren't my strengths," Missy says.

As a divorced single mother of two children, Missy didn't have time to go back to school. She needed help she could fit into her busy schedule.

Controlling the Financials

Bill Love,
managing partner,
W.P. Love Parners.
BioSystems, CEO

In 2002, she joined HEMP, hoping her mentor Bill Love would guide her business to the next level. But first, they had to come to a meeting of the minds.

"Until my mentor entered the picture, our business had literally been all in the family. My father just about fell off his chair when I told him I was giving a stranger three years' worth of financial statements," Missy says.

Bill reviewed the statements and returned with a twenty-page analysis.

"I'm looking at what's on my desk and he's looking at my business from twenty-five thousand feet in the air," Missy recalls. "I knew so little that his analysis was over my head. I struggled to understand what he was talking about."

After the HEMP director talked to Bill, he focused on communicating simply and clearly. They both committed to regular meeting times and the mentoring relationship began to really work. With guidance from her mentor, Missy learned to understand financial statements and started to review expenses regularly.

Bill also took an in-depth look at her business, spending time in different departments and pointing out areas of strengths and weakness. He helped her more thoroughly define some of the business's key roles and encouraged her to assign those employees more responsibility.

Designing Functional Processes

Bill also encouraged her to create procedures and devise a percentage of sales for each product line.

"I studied trends in my business," Missy says. "If I was selling 70 percent mink, I didn't need to spend so much time buying leather. Once I learned to equate the percentage of sales to dollars, I had more of a sense of what to buy and manufacture."

She also learned to relinquish some control and get her staff more involved in buying and manufacturing decisions. As she traveled the world on buying trips, she photographed potential products, creating a catalogue for her managers.

"They could see everything we might make or buy next year and give me feedback on various products," she says. "I also visited our manufacturing plants and took pictures of different styles. Through staff input, we might change a collar, color, or length. Getting more help from my staff improved morale and helped product flow."

Love Prevails

During the mentoring process, Bill and Missy became friends. Several months after she graduated from HEMP, Bill asked her out on a date.

Because of their business interactions, the two already had great respect for each other. The date went well and they continued to see each other. Three years later, they were married. They count themselves as one of HEMP's extremely successful "matches."

The Replay

THE SITUATION:

Missy didn't understand the financial foundation of her business.

- She wanted to grow the business but didn't know how to read a financial statement.
- She had had no training on forecasting or budgeting.
- She was involved in a family business that was used to doing things a certain way.

THE SOLUTION:

- Know your own weaknesses and reach out for help from a variety of experts.
- Ask questions until you understand financial statements and budgeting process.
- Define the roles of your key personnel.
- Be willing to let go of the familiar and embrace new ideas and improvements.

THE RESULTS:

Missy builds her knowledge base, relinquishes some control, and creates processes and procedures to reduce expenses and improve business.

- Staff has increased autonomy and responsibility.
- Missy can now spend time diversifying the product line and exploring venues for expanding the business.
- Missy is now married to a wonderful man.

Deuce Livers and Livers Bronze:

TAKING THE BRONZE AND STRENGTHENING THE FAMILY BUSINESS

Photo by Bruce Mathews.

"How many family members are in this business?" Ray Pitman asked Deuce (Richard) Livers at one of their early mentoring meetings.

"Eight," Deuce replied.

"Ten percent of your staff is related," Ray observed. "You have a lot to work on!"

As the new president of his family's business, Livers Bronze, Deuce was well aware he had a lot to learn.

"I didn't really know what being president meant," Deuce says.

His dad and uncles started Livers Bronze in 1946 and Deuce had grown up in the business. Summers, he and his brothers worked where they were needed, either the machine shop, foundry, or the assembly department. The company specialized in ornamental metals

Ray Pitman,
founder,
Pitman Manufacturing,
RO Corporation

and innovative hand railing systems and their products graced commercial buildings throughout Kansas City.

After high school, Deuce went to the University of Missouri, Columbia, and then transferred to Longview Community College to complete an Associate's degree, before returning to work at Livers.

When his father stepped down and his siblings asked him to become president, Deuce returned to college to earn a BA. For eight years, he attended night school at Avila University. Part of that time, he was participating in HEMP and four of his children were also in college!

"I had been involved in plant operations, scheduling, field operations, and human resources," Deuce says. "But as president, I knew I needed to drag myself out of the details and look at the business from the higher point of view."

He knew he needed help. Even after he received his degree, he continued searching for a group that could help him more fully understand how to be an effective leader and how to take his company to the next level.

Finding Help and Improving Communications

"I found the place we've been looking for," his long-time friend Mary Lou Jacoby, owner, Warehouse 1, said when she called Deuce that spring of 2000.

She took him to a HEMP event and Deuce realized he had found his potential support group.

"This was a unique set of people from all sorts of businesses," he says. "I applied to become a mentee and was admitted to the program."

His mentor, Ray Pitman, quickly endeared himself to Deuce's brothers and sisters and began helping Deuce hone his leadership skills.

"Maintaining a family business requires a lot of good communication," Ray said. "You can't be democratic; you have to become more decisive. Everyone looks up to a leader."

Deuce had a tendency to communicate indirectly. He had to train himself to say what was on his mind in the right way. In the beginning of the mentoring process, some family members worked through Ray to communicate with Deuce.

"They didn't feel comfortable talking to me about things such as salary issues and interpersonal family conflicts," Deuce admits. "They went to Ray, Ray talked to me, and then I talked to my family."

Deuce worked on communicating more directly and effectively.

"Now we can talk to each other about anything," Deuce says.

That was just the beginning of the changes Deuce would make.

Knowing What You've Sold

Deuce had worked in operations all his life and had never been involved in sales and marketing.

"You need to know what you're selling and connect sales to the rest of the business," Ray advised.

They worked on developing organization charts and created the concept of project management teams.

"Through organizing in this way, we changed our whole structure," Deuce says. "Originally, the sales team had a scratch-pad approach to estimating. We automated the estimating process and moved it over to the engineering department."

The sales team focused on closing the sales.

Making these major changes was not easy. There was a lot of internal protesting and resistance and Deuce and his management team really worked with the employees to make the transitions smooth.

The results changed the scope of Livers Bronze. Today, the company has four estimators, who work in engineering under the IT person. The estimators use sophisticated electronic tools that allow them to bid a hundred jobs a month. They feed those statistics to the sales staff, which creates a sales proposal and tries to close the deal.

"Streamlining this process has increased our sales," Deuce says. "Now, we can deliver prices quickly and use our estimates as a marketing tool."

Marketing the Core

Instead of expanding, Deuce focused on marketing his core product. Working with marketing experts he'd met through HEMP, the company did its first mass mailing and had its website rebuilt.

Through networking at HEMP, Deuce learned that one of the HEMPers owned an overseas company that did programming work and offered the services of qualified AutoCAD engineers, who could quickly produce and transmit approval drawings, which are the initial drawings the client sees.

"We'd had a hard time finding AutoCAD professionals in the U.S.," Deuce says. "The ability to quickly generate approval drawings rejuvenated our sales."

Lenda and Deuce Livers with Sharon and Lirel Holt enjoy a quiet moment.

Once again, Deuce segmented the process, using the overseas resources for initial drawings and his Kansas City crew for production drawings.

"Separating numerous aspects of estimating and production reduces stress, increases flexibility, and improves our market presence," Deuce says.

BUILDING A TEAM AND DEEPENING THE CULTURE

Following Ray's suggestion, Deuce put together an executive team with the key people in the business, including nonfamily members. Every month, they have a lunch meeting and every quarter they host an all-employee celebration lunch.

"Everyone participates in that quarterly lunch, so it's not me just running the show," Deuce says.

His sister talks about the financial performance, his brothers talk about sales and marketing, and the IT and materials people discuss aspects of their operations. This quarterly gathering brings everyone together and strengthens the company culture.

Estimating the Future

Deuce's vision for the future includes investing in technology and aligning the right machinery with the right people.

His focus is unusual. "I want to do a better job of connecting our engineering department with our shop, so we can more quickly turn out better product," Deuce says.

That means everyone will know how the product is drawn, produced, shipped, and installed.

"Once we accomplish that, there'll be no stopping us," Deuce says. "With such transparency, our staff will be able to offer ideas for improvements and we'll instantly know if something is going wrong."

Deuce feels participating in HEMP was a turning point in his life.

"The whole HEMP experience was incredible," he says. "For three years, I went to classes, read eye-opening books, and worked with a mentor. You can't find that kind of training anywhere else."

Though Deuce is not a micromanager, he now knows everything that is going on in his business.

"With that knowledge, I can more effectively run the company and keep everyone together," he says.

THE SITUATION:

Deuce Livers didn't really know what it meant to be president of his family business.

- He'd worked in the operational part of the business his whole life.
- He didn't understand marketing or sales.
- He wasn't comfortable communicating directly with his family members.

THE SOLUTION:

- Analyze business processes and look for ways to segment and streamline.
- Know what you're selling and connect sales to the rest of the company.
- Become a decision maker and a direct communicator.

THE RESULTS:

Deuce reorganizes the business, expanding the company's sales and production abilities.

- He automates the estimating process, increasing the accuracy and swiftness of the bids.
- He goes beyond the informal family system and segments aspects of the business for greater flexibility, marketability, and profitability.
- He creates an integrated vision for his company's future.

Jason Collene and Collene Concrete:

BUILDING A FOCUSED FOUNDATION

COLLENE CONCRETE

913-788-4600

3500

colleneconcrete.com

USDOT 926610

"You are going to make it," Ray Pitman assured Jason Collene. "I've seen businesses in much worse shape."

That fall of 2008, Collene Concrete was in trouble. Several years earlier, in an effort to expand, Jason's brother had joined the company and had taken on full-scope concrete contracting work in addition to the flat concrete work Jason excelled at.

"We did not do the contracting well and I was in over my head," Jason says. "I hired too many people and felt I'd lost control of the company. I hoped HEMP would help me."

But Jason's first mentor was a broad-picture person. Jason was looking for concrete answers, literally and figuratively, and he was receiving vagaries.

Concerned that his business wouldn't make it through the winter, he turned to Ray Pitman, whom he'd met at HEMP gatherings.

Ray had a wealth of experience in solving business problems and instantly gave Jason practical advice.

Ray Pitman,
founder,
Pitman Manufacturing,
RO Corporation

"Here are the things you need to do today before you leave the office," Ray told him. "You have no money coming in, so you can't spend any more money. You have to let go of six office people. You need to temporarily stop the projects that are draining your financial resources. And you need to lay off several work crews for a week."

It was hard for Jason to let go of his employees, but he listened to Ray's advice. Three of his office staff volunteered to stay on without pay for a couple of weeks, to help Jason get through the crisis.

Bringing SWOT to the Rescue

Within a day, Ray called together a SWOT team (Strengths Weaknesses Opportunities Threats), of six business professionals to help Jason further problem solve.

Dan McDougal,
president/CEO of
Dredge America

"I was running out of capital, "Jason says. "The team went through my financials and showed me where I was losing money and told me what I needed to do to stop the bleeding."

They advised Jason to approach multiple banks, in an effort to secure additional capital. But he was already in debt and the construction industry was slowing down. No one wanted to loan him money.

HEMP arranged for a new mentor, Dan McDougal, president/CEO of Dredge America. Dan looked over everything Jason was doing and helped him devise a survival plan. He suggested Jason ask a trusted supplier for a loan, since the banks weren't interested. Jason did and that loan got him through the most difficult weeks.

"Dan's perspective was wide," Jason says. "He'd been through tough times and he helped me see all the opportunities."

Even with those opportunities, it was a stressful period. Jason had to constantly negotiate with suppliers, trying to make ends meet.

"At the end of every week, I felt hopeless and knew there was no way I could get through this," Jason says. "But Dan and Ray and other HEMPers kept encouraging me, saying, 'I know you can do it.'"

That encouragement gave him the strength to press through the adversity.

"It's taken the three years of my HEMP training to implement our plan," Jason says.

The plan focused on where the company made money. Dan suggested Jason concentrate on just doing concrete flatwork. He guided Jason in looking for ways to get more jobs that were profitable. Then, Jason had to start cutting away the rest of the company. During the next year and a half, the company went from sixty-five people to thirteen people.

"That included letting my brother go, which was hard," Jason says.

Pouring the Original Foundation

Jason had grown up doing construction and foundation repair.

An uncle did commercial flatwork, pouring concrete slabs for buildings, sidewalks, and curbs. When Jason was eighteen, he lived with this uncle for a couple of years.

"He was my boot camp when I was going through a rebellious period," Jason says. "I learned the field concrete side of the business."

He also learned his uncle's old-school business model: "You do the work and hire the least amount of people possible."

After he left his uncle's company, Jason worked as a foreman on a variety of projects. But he didn't enjoy taking instructions from other people. In 1999, when he was twenty-seven years old, he took on side jobs as a concrete finisher. Those jobs grew into Collene Concrete.

For the first six months, Jason worked solo, calling in concrete finishers when he needed help pouring. As business increased, he hired field and office staffs.

"I had high aspirations for the company," he says. "I kept pursuing bigger jobs and commercial work."

By the end of the second year, he had six employees and was doing quite a bit of commercial work. His brother had an expertise in general contracting and came on as a project manager. With the addition of the contracting business, the company grew. But instead of becoming more profitable, Jason felt the company was imploding. Quality went down as did employee loyalty.

Refocusing on Flatwork

During his time in HEMP, Dan helped strategize for the future, asking Jason, "Where do you want to go?"

Initially, Jason didn't really know the answer. With Dan's guidance, he changed his focus from quantity to quality.

"I was bidding against other companies, trying to compete in a tight market," Jason says. "We were losing money on the general contracting jobs."

Still, refocusing the company and concentrating only on flatwork was one of Jason's most difficult and important decisions.

"That was a turning point for me," Jason says. "Now, I'm doing a different kind of flatwork than I started out with. We do 95 percent renovation and tear-out replacement work."

Jason focuses on the Kansas City market. A national convenience store is his biggest client and every day Jason's crews tear out and replace at area stores. He seeks other similar clients and devotes time to customer service and marketing.

Pushing Through to Success

"Now, I'm actually having fun," Jason says. "I wake up knowing what I'm doing and what my goals are. I have a crew of fifteen loyal and hard-working men who are proud of the work they do."

During the three years in HEMP, Jason learned how much perseverance and grit he had. He learned that sometimes success means just pushing through and sticking with it.

"I also had to let go of my pride and really listen to other people," he says.

He discarded his uncle's old world "Do all the work yourself" business model and embraced the HEMP creed of working on instead of in the company.

"I'm now focused and profitable and that makes a world of difference," he says.

The Replay

THE SITUATION:

Jason Collene had expanded his business and lost control of quality and profits.

- He was bidding against others in a tight market.
- He had hired the wrong people and quality control had decreased.
- He didn't have a vision or direction for the business.

THE SOLUTIONS:

- Stop spending and start focusing.
- Cut down staff.
- Look for the profit centers.
- Concentrate on what you're good at.

THE RESULTS:

Jason moves through the tough times and refocuses his business.

- He has a loyal work crew and a top-quality product.
- He works on the business strategically, looking for the right kinds of clients.
- He let go of the old-school business model and is now enjoying his business.

Photo by Bruce Mathews.

Joe Runyan and Hangers Cleaners:

CLEANING UP THE PROFITABILITY

"Are you kidding me?" Joe Runyan stood in the dingy dry cleaners, staring at the bright white button shining out from the middle of his dark green shirt.

"A button fell off and we replaced it," the clerk told him.

"The other buttons are dark green," Joe said.

"All right, sir, we'll fix this."

A week later, Joe picked up his shirt. He couldn't believe what he saw—all the buttons were bright white!

He decided to change dry cleaners. He shopped around and was dismayed at the low level of customer service. It was the late 1990s and Joe, age thirty-three, was working for Sprint. He liked his job but he knew the company was down-sizing. He'd been thinking about starting his own business and this incongruous white button sparked his entrepreneurial spirit.

He looked into the dry cleaning industry, but didn't like the idea of using the harsh chemicals that seemed inherent to the cleaning process. Still, the idea simmered in the back of his mind.

Discovering the CO2 Factor

In spring 2002, Joe was on a business trip in Minnesota. After work, he joined a co-worker and her engineer husband for a drink.

"Talking to the husband was like pulling teeth," Joe recalls. He kept asking the guy questions and finally stumbled upon an interesting topic.

"Our company has just developed a patent for an effective and eco-friendly CO2 cleaning agent that will revolutionize dry cleaning," the husband told him.

Joe sat up straighter. He asked to have the patent information sent to him.

Back home, Joe began developing a business plan. The process was daunting; he was starting from scratch and needed real estate, equipment, staff, knowledge, and operating capital.

Meanwhile, Sprint was continuing layoffs. In October, Joe told his boss he was open to considering a severance package, figuring he'd have at least six more months on the job. Ten days later, his boss called and said, "You're gone."

Joe was scared. His wife told him, "Pursue your dream. Our kids are young. They're not going to know if we're poor."

Looking for Dirty Laundry

Joe raised money, leased a building in Kansas City, Missouri, bought equipment from a defunct dry cleaner in North Carolina, and worked doggedly to set up the complicated infrastructure of a dry cleaning plant.

The Hangers Cleaners plant, complete with a customer service counter, opened in Kansas City in January 2004.

Then came the big question: Where was the dirty laundry?

Joe wanted to set up a retail store in the thriving Brookside area of Kansas City, Missouri. But the leasing agent wouldn't rent Joe space. There was another cleaner in the area, he said. Plus the agent felt a new business with an inexperienced operator might be a financial risk.

"That rejection made me feel frustrated and angry," Joe says. "So I bought a van, hired a driver, and drove through Brookside, offering free pick-up and delivery and ecologically friendly cleaning."

The concept worked. A good dry cleaning store takes several years to build up to an annual gross of $200,000 to $300,000. Within ninety days, the first Hangers Cleaners route was doing the equivalent of an annualized $300,000.

"I knew we were onto something," Joe says.

He bought another van and another. When the business was six months old, Joe heard that a local store director in one Hy-Vee grocery chain was dissatisfied with his current dry cleaning vendor. Joe offered to simplify the store's dry cleaning processing, making life easier for the Hy-Vee employees who worked with dry cleaning.

He got the contract.

"Hy-Vee was a great partner," Joe says. "Plus, having our brand associated with them really legitimized our business."

A year later, Hangers Cleaners was supplying dry cleaning services to eight additional area Hy-Vee's.

Joe continued to expand his pick-up and delivery routes, traveling throughout the Kansas City area and into Lawrence and DeSoto, Kansas. He made it easy for home delivery customer: Hangers kept their credit card information on file. The customer put out their laundry for pick-up and when it was returned, Hangers simply charged their credit card.

"In a retail store, customers can go for weeks or months without picking up their clothes," Joe says. "With the delivery business, the cash flow is much stronger."

But not strong enough. Even though the business was grossing a million a year, Hangers was not profitable.

"We were serving too large an area and we were bleeding cash," Joe says.

Finding the Routes to Growth

Joe had poured everything he had into the business and had exhausted his options for borrowing money.

"I didn't understand how to grow profitably," he says.

He stopped taking salary and lived on his 401k from Sprint. He had built up credit card debt. Each time he scraped together more money, he thought, "Success is just around the corner."

But the corner didn't show up. Debt, stress, and uncertainty ate at him. He lay awake in bed, praying and hoping Hy-Vee would send a payment so he could make the payroll.

In 2005, when a colleague mentioned HEMP, Joe was eager to get involved in the program.

Mentor Melody Warren, president and CEO, Transportation Logistics Systems, quickly began learning about Joe's business.

She asked him questions, such as: "Why are you serving Lawrence? Where do you make money? What do you do well? What do you not do well?"

"We looked at the business with a fine-tooth comb," Joe says. "Our expenses were in line with industry norms. But with Melody's help, I realized I was spreading myself too thin and spending money in areas I didn't need to serve."

He stopped going to Lawrence and DeSoto. He kept all his vans and drivers but reduced their geographic areas, cutting back on gas expense and drive time.

Joe did a SWOT (Strengths, Weaknesses, Opportunities, Threats) analysis on the business and on himself, which helped him notice the kinds of tasks he avoided doing.

"I don't like conflict and I'm not good at delegating," he admits. "If someone wasn't doing his job, I wouldn't address the issue. I'd fume and boil and then I'd go do the work. I realized I couldn't grow the business if I didn't change that behavior."

The business also lacked procedures.

Melody Warren,
president and CEO,
Transportation
Logistics Systems

"I expected people to know what to do and then I'd get frustrated when they didn't understand the system," he says.

With his mentor's guidance, he and his team documented processes and made sure employees understood their jobs. As he honed the procedures, Hangers' efficiency improved.

Avoiding Being Taken to the Cleaners

A year into his mentoring process, Joe learned a national company was coming to Kansas City to set up a number of dry cleaning outlets. Joe worried such competition would put him out of business. He did another SWOT analysis and asked the question, "What can we do that a big national company cannot?"

Hangers couldn't compete in research, marketing, or beautiful retail stores. But the company could compete in the way it connected with and talked to its customers.

"At that time, our business communication was bland and professional," Joe says. "We decided to create a playful edge and have fun talking to our customers."

Joe let out his natural wit and humor. When Hangers sent funny emails, customers instantly responded. "I was having a bad day and your email made me feel good," one customer wrote.

"Can you imagine? A dry cleaner made him feel good!" Joe says. "The threat of competition helped us find our unique voice."

Growing into Profitability

Today the company is still growing and is profitable. It's received multiple awards for its eco-friendly practices and for its excellent customer service.

"I feel excited when I walk through this company and think, 'There are thirty-one jobs here because of that stupid white button,'" Joe says.

The Replay

THE SITUATION:

Joe Runyan did not know how to grow and remain profitable.

- He expanded territory without analyzing market viability.
- His means of borrowing money were exhausted.
- He was grossing a million dollars annually and not making a profit. He felt he was bleeding cash.

THE SOLUTION:

- Do a SWOT analysis of the business and of the entrepreneur.
- Ask tough questions and be willing to change.
- Pare down unprofitable services as a way to contain spending.
- Fine-tune customer communications, using a witty, unique voice.
- Find and focus on your strengths.

THE RESULTS:

Joe has grown the company and the bottom line.

- Hangers has grown from six to thirty-one employees.
- The company now grosses more than $1.5 million and is profitable.
- Joe is happier running his business, because he has procedures and systems in place.

Photo by Bruce Mathews.

Neal Sharma and Digital Evolution Group:

MAKING THE MOST
OF PEERS
AND MENTORS

When Neal Sharma joined the HEMP program in 2004, he was twenty-seven years old and the co-owner of the three-year-old Digital Evolution Group, a full-service digital consultancy that developed Internet-focused marketing and business solutions.

Mentors Molded the Man

Neal had experienced many mentors in his life and believed that there were three components of mentorship: advice, encouragement, and exposure.

"As an entrepreneur, it's easy to be insular," Neal says. "You need someone to show you how to look at various aspects of your business. Ideally, a mentor fills the critical knowledge gap."

He had grown up in Syracuse, Kansas. Neal's mother, a physician in private practice, served as an early mentor and role model.

"Your word is your bond," she told him. "Hard work and focused effort will pay more dividends than anything else."

Neal's first business was selling stickers to other third graders.

"I'd give them one and I'd get two back," he says. "When they asked why they had to give me two, I told them I needed to make a profit."

At age fourteen, he moved with his family to the Kansas City area. One summer, while still in high school, Neal developed a discount card for people who worked downtown, partnering with downtown restaurants on a "buy-one, get-one-free" lunch program. He stood on the street corners and in office buildings, selling his discount card. The venture was a success.

"I made more money than I spent," he says.

The summer between his freshman and sophomore year at American University in Washington, D.C., he was licensed as a commercial real estate broker. When he resumed school, he formed a web development firm that was an early version of his current company. He operated that business from his dorm room. When he had a chance to work on Senator Bob Dole's 1996 presidential campaign, he stayed in school but let go of his business.

"When the campaign ended, I plunged back into my studies and rescued my grades," Neal says.

He went to business school at the University of Kansas as a graduate student and was serving as student body president of the MBA program when Cheryl Womack came to speak to his class. Cheryl was a ground-breaking entrepreneur who founded VCW Holding Companies, offering insurance and other services for the independent trucking industry. Her story of rising up and starting her own business inspired Neal. The two of them became friends. Cheryl was an important mentor, connector, and also an initial investor in Digital Evolution Group.

As he grew his business, Neal frequently turned to people for advice.

"When my partner and I started the business, we went to lunch with different business people, seeking insights and advice. I gained ten pounds trying to learn the things I didn't know yet."

Each of his mentors reminded Neal: "You don't have all the answers and you don't need to have all the answers. That's where mentors can help you."

Finding the Smart People

HEMP brought him both peers and mentors.

Initially, he dismissed a piece of advice from Barnett Helzberg: "You should surround yourself with people smarter than you."

"I didn't know what that meant," he says. "I thought Barnett was being humble."

Then, during Lunch with the Big Guy, Neal had an "aha!" moment. Barnett told this story:

"I was involved in every one of our store's leases. Then we hired a vice president of real estate, someone who was far smarter than I was on the subject. When the new VP began

Barnett Helzberg,
chairman and founder of HEMP

making the real estate decisions, our company really started to grow dramatically."

As Barnett's story sank in, Neal realized he didn't have to know and control everything his business did. He stopped trying to learn all the new technology and started hiring technology experts.

"My desire to know how everything works might have actually slowed the company's growth," he says. "Now I have experts in these areas. Since I've stopped trying to be good at every function, I've become better at leading people and articulating the vision."

A HEMP peer gave him another leadership idea, by saying, "When a new associate is hired, I sit with them and tell them our mission, our vision, and our core values."

That resonated with Neal. But first he had to articulate his core values.

"Until then, we were just a bunch of people running a business," Neal says.

He reached out to the staff and asked," What do you think we stand for? What kind of company do you want to work for?"

From those responses, an ad-hoc committee defined the company's core values.

"We've since hired dozens of people," Neal says. "I meet with each one personally on the first day of employment and talk about what we stand for and our values. I manage from these values."

Lessons Learned

Neal Sharma continues to benefit from his HEMP experiences and from other business mentors. He's constantly listening and learning.

"I don't expect to be the best," he says, "simply because 'best' is a relative notion. But I do want to be excellent, because 'excellent' does not depend upon anyone else. Excellent is objective."

THE SITUATION:

Neal Sharma wanted to become a better businessman, entrepreneur, and manager.

- He wanted to avoid the isolation and singularity that can come from being an entrepreneur.
- He wanted to expand his exposure and viewpoint by connecting with mentors and peers.
- He wanted to grow his company and improve his managerial skills.

THE SOLUTION:

- Reach out to a variety of people for advice.
- Hire more experts and focus on the larger picture.
- Involve staff and identify the core values of his company.
- Communicate those values to each new employee and use them as a management tool.

THE RESULTS:

Neal has hired experts and now uses the core values as an effective management tool.

- All employees know and understand the importance of those values.
- The business continues to flourish and grow.

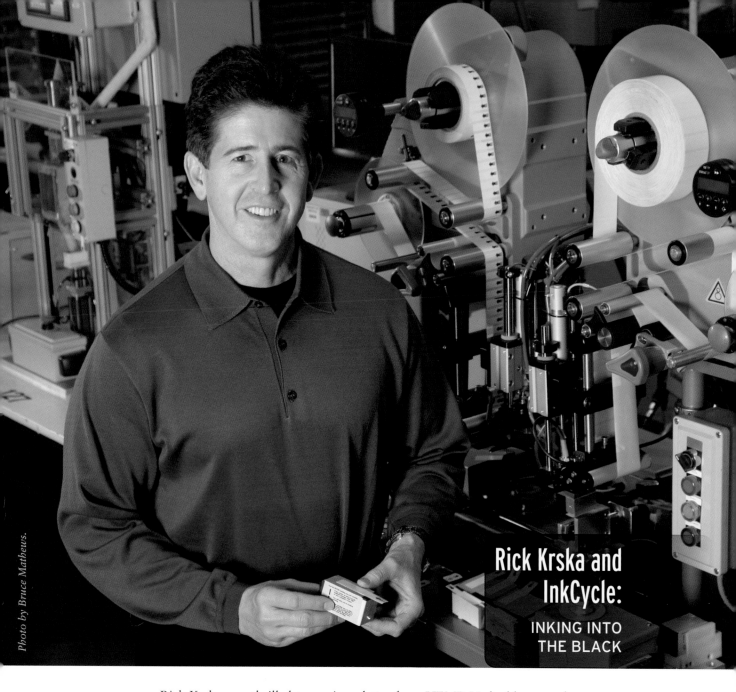

Photo by Bruce Mathews.

Rick Krska and InkCycle:
INKING INTO THE BLACK

Rick Krska was thrilled to receive a letter from HEMP. He had been a salesman at Helzberg Diamonds when he was in college, but he had never met Barnett Helzberg. Now, Helzberg was inviting Krska to apply to the entrepreneurial mentoring program.

Rick, age thirty-five, was ready for mentoring. It was 1995 and his company, InkCycle, which produced and distributed aftermarket toners and cartridges, was three years old. The company had recently moved into an 8,500 square-foot factory. Rick had twenty people working for him and was doing about a million dollars a year in sales.

"I was seeking additional wisdom and knowledge and I wanted to connect with other business people," Rick says.

The Early Entrepreneur

From an early age, Rick expressed his entrepreneurial spirit. He built his paper route from twenty-five to three hundred subscribers. He started mowing lawns and ended up buying mowers and hiring other kids.

"I had a brand new car at age sixteen that I paid for," he says.

In high school, he bought old houses, rehabbed them, and sold them.

"I loved creating a business," Rick says.

Rick attended Longview Community College in Lee's Summit, Missouri, to get some basic business skills, then went to work in the nuclear weapons industry at Allied Signal, in Kansas City, Missouri.

"There I learned I loved manufacturing and I loved building a team," he says. In 1992, he began looking for an entrepreneurial opportunity. He heard about an ink recycling business for sale, but the deal didn't work out. Still, the idea really appealed to him.

"I liked the industry," Rick says. "I liked the consumable part, the technology and manufacturing aspects, and the green component. Plus, everyone used ink cartridges."

Then he saw an ad in the back of *Entrepreneur* magazine that sparked his interest: a training course in remanufacturing toner cartridges and repairing laser printers. Rick went to Texas and took the training. In 1992, at the age of thirty-two, he started InkCycle in his basement.

Becoming Chief Executive Servant

By day, Rick continued his full-time job. By night, he grew his fledgling company. His wife helped him with the paperwork. A former employee joined the venture, handing out business cards and brochures during the day, then working with Rick to fill orders at night. As the company grew, they worked later and later on past midnight. The business outgrew the basement, then spread through the family room. Once it spilled over into the rest of the house, Rick moved into a factory space.

Rick's father, a lumberjack and sheet metalworker, had been Rick's first mentor. He gave his son this piece of advice: "If you want to create something significant, you need to ask, 'How am I going to serve and make peoples' lives better?'"

Early on, Rick took the title of chief executive servant.

A Life-Changing Visit

Barnett Helzberg walked into the back door of InkCycle's factory. He talked to Rick's employees and looked around. Then he sat in the office with Rick.

"Your employees really love you and love the company," Barnett told Rick in the fall of 1995. "You're going to be a $100-million business one day. I want to be your mentor."

"That was a great day in my life," Rick says.

Barnett encouraged Rick to have more than one mentor. He also urged Rick to join the Young Presidents Organization, a worldwide organization that educates and connects CEOs. That organization provided Rick with a group of peers that met monthly. The HEMP community was another rich resource. At one meeting, Rick met Linda Gill Taylor, an entrepreneur who had started a company that offered professional temp services to lawyers.

Linda Gill Taylor,
executive director,
the Center for the City
at UMKC

"I was blown away with how smart she was," he says. "I slipped her a note and asked if she would also be my mentor."

She said yes.

At one mentoring meeting, Linda told Rick, "I am going to take you around and introduce you to some important Kansas City people."

Those introductions built Rick's knowledge and his base of friends, and they boosted his business.

Learning to Quick-Fire

During the mentoring process, InkCycle made a lot of changes, including adding an advisory board, upgrading its human resources department, and improving sales and marketing.

"We went from doing things in a small way and getting by on luck to a more conscious and structured approach," Rick says. "We also added in a training component."

With his mentors' help, Rick changed how he dealt with his employees.

"I had the wrong people in certain jobs," Rick says.

One day he called Barnett for advice, saying "I need to do something with this troublesome employee. He's my friend and I don't want to fire this guy."

"You have to do what's right for the rest of the employees," Barnett said. He gave Rick this piece of advice: "Hire slowly and fire quickly."

Rick took the advice. The next time he faced such an issue, he remembered Barnett's words and moved swiftly on his own.

Calls and Questions That Strengthened Business

As Rick listened to his mentors and other HEMPers, he gradually became comfortable letting go of some of his control and delegating more.

"I still wanted to be grounded in the company details but I learned to see myself as a source of influence rather than control," he says.

He also learned to seek information from his employees. Using a model from Ted Cohn, a friend of HEMP and author of *Management Smarts*, Rick instituted a year-end employee meeting. There he asked his employees questions such as:

- What do you want to be when you grow up?
- If you were president of the company, what would you change?
- Are you being paid fairly?

He was pleased to hear that most of his employees were satisfied with their pay. He listened carefully to their comments and suggestions.

"When I heard something that resonated, I incorporated it," he says.

One employee told Rick, "I'm not being paid fairly. I'm working beyond what you hired me to do and I should be paid more."

When Rick learned about all the additional work this employee was doing, he arranged for a commensurate pay raise.

Often his questions opened up a valuable dialogue, where the employees asked questions and learned more about the business.

"My management style is wandering around and talking to people," Rick says. "I get a lot of important information from my conversations."

One of his board members suggested that Rick call his suppliers once a year, to tell them how much he appreciated them.

"The connections I built from those phone calls made a big difference when I was later negotiating with the vendors," he says.

Barnett suggested Rick call his customers every year.

"Ask them, 'What are we doing that you like? What are we doing that you don't like? What are we not doing that you would like us to do?'"

Rick made the calls and instantly received a $10,000 order.

Surviving the Challenges

In 1995, when Rick joined HEMP, he had twenty-five employees. Within ten years, the company had grown rapidly and employed eight hundred people.

"During that period of growth, it was important to have mentors," Rick says.

Then, in 2006, Rick received a phone call that changed his life. One of his big customers altered its ordering pattern and Rick had to suddenly shrink his workforce to two hundred employees.

Devastated, Rick told Barnett what had happened.

"Congratulations," Barnett said. "You're being kicked upstairs."

"I feel like I'm being kicked in the gut," Rick replied.

"You're being forced to reorganize and you're going to become a better company," Barnett said.

Rick left, comforted by the feedback, ready to rebuild his business. Today, he's worked to create a more diverse customer base.

"My new mantra is, 'Be a servant to many and a slave to none,'" Rick says.

Asking for the Help You Need

Rick gained enormously from the mentoring experience because he asked for help when he needed it. His mentors benefited from seeing him follow through on their suggestions.

"When I started a business I had no idea that successful people would want to help me for free," Rick says. "Their generosity changed the way I looked at the world."

The Replay

THE SITUATION:

Rick Krska was seeking business wisdom and connections.
- He was doing things in a small way, relying on luck rather than structure.
- He had the wrong people in certain jobs.
- He wasn't part of the business networking community.

THE SOLUTION:
- Create a structure independent of the entrepreneur.
- Heed the advice, "Hire slowly. Fire quickly."
- Talk to the employees; ask their advice and listen to their feedback.
- Create strong relationships with vendors.
- Seek wisdom and mentoring from many.

THE RESULTS:

Rick improves his business and has enough flexibility to weather serious income fluctuations.
- Rick grew the business during good times and is able to guide his business through an economic downturn.
- His ability to connect and listen to people solidifies his work force and builds strong vendor relationships.

YOUR MULTI-CHANNEL MARKETING

YOUR PATRONS WHERE THEY ARE

Mobile & Text

Twitter

QR Codes & Short URLs

Facebook

Wi-Fi Hot Spots

Landing Pages & Mobile Pages

emfLUENCE
Interactive Marketing

Dave Cacioppo and Emfluence:

TARGETING TECHNOLOGY AND CUSTOMER SERVICE

Photo by Bruce Mathews.

CHRW Advertising was lucky—the full-service ad agency was doing well even though its four principals didn't know their way around a financial statement and hadn't a clue about human resources.

Their goal was to do great work for clients and offer generous benefits to their employees.

"But we had no idea how to deal with benefits or human resource issues," says Dave Cacioppo, who was the most technically oriented of the partners. "We were just four creative guys who were semi-clueless about running a business."

They'd started the company in 1999 as equal partners. In 2003, they added Emfluence, a digital component to the business. Dave was highly involved with Emfluence, which specialized in web-development services and email marketing.

Dave had heard of HEMP years earlier, when he'd played a small part in developing a brochure for the program as an employee at Bernstein-Rein Advertising.

"I've never been afraid to ask for help," he says. "If something is going wrong, I own it and talk it through. My personality type is, 'Holy crap. I have a problem. Let's fix it.'"

When a friend suggested Dave join HEMP, the idea aligned with his thinking. His partners approved and Dave welcomed the chance to have access to HEMP's experienced mentors.

Getting Organized and Automated

Dave's mentor, Mike O'Malley, a CPA with a specialty in mergers and acquisitions, was the perfect match.

First, he helped the partners define their specific roles in the business, eliminating the necessity for so many decisions by committee.

Dave and his partners had started the company with the mantra, "Just do a great job for the clients." But they weren't asking: "Did we bid the job properly? Did we lose money getting the client a great product?"

"We suspected we were losing money on bids," Dave says. "But we didn't know what to do about the problem."

Through analyzing the financials, Mike identified the issues and explained how they were underbidding projects. He also reviewed CHRW's expensive health care benefits and offered suggestions for reducing the costs, while still offering excellent employee benefits.

Mike O'Malley,
*President,
O'Keeffe & O'Malley,
Inc.*

Dave saw the value of Mike's suggestions. He organized the financial statements and reviewed them on a regular basis. He also listened carefully as Mike and HEMP leaders emphasized hiring the best people for the job. He developed solid interviewing procedures, including personality profiles. He went beyond looking for a good employee and began consciously seeking the best person for each position.

Merging and Separating

One of their long-time clients, a Lawrence-based ad agency that CHRW did contract work for, landed a large account and needed to grow quickly to fulfill it. The agency approached CHRW and asked, "Would you like to be acquired?"

Mike talked to all the principals, asking each what he wanted from a possible merger.

"I feel the digital side of our business is undervalued by this agency," Dave told Mike. "Emfluence has great technology with massive potential. In a perfect world, I would keep the technology and digital side and not go with the merger."

The others agreed and Dave kept Emfluence. Turning down the merger was a pivotal point for Dave.

Initially, Dave's transition from partner to business owner was challenging. Because he no longer had the resources of the agency, his staff and revenues were cut. Emfluence also faced the daunting prospect of a multi-year lease that CHRW no longer partially covered. Following Mike's advice, Dave reached out to his landlord and renegotiated the lease, so his payments were 30 percent lower.

Financials were not Dave's strong suit and he struggled as Mike guided him through the difficult process of breaking his core services into individual profit centers, each with

Dave Cacioppo, Dan McDougal, and John Vandewalle enjoy the food.

its own P&L. It took a lot of analysis to decide how to track and allocate overhead to the appropriate centers, but once the work was done, the results were invaluable.

"We knew exactly how each of our offerings was performing," Dave says. "We've maintained and refined that system and it has helped immensely when it comes to staffing and other decisions."

Every month, Dave reviewed each of his six profit centers and asked, "How is this area performing and what can make it better?"

He carried that focus on data into his client work. "We are results-driven for the client as well." Dave says. "I can show the client how we are helping them make money."

Making the Most of HEMP Resources

Even after he finished the formal mentoring part of the program, Dave stayed involved with HEMP, becoming a Fellow, serving as the Board's marketing chair and helping with web development. He readily shared his knowledge of digital marketing and continued to benefit from the powerful HEMP resource network.

In 2008, Emfluence had invited two thousand people to a large outdoor party. The day of the event, major storms were slated to come through Kansas City. Though normally a quick decision-maker, Dave couldn't decide whether he should cancel the party. He wrestled with the pros and cons until he remembered a HEMPer, Sara Croke, president of Weather or Not, Inc., who offered pinpoint weather accuracy.

"I called and asked her what we should do," he says. "She produced an amazingly accurate and detailed forecast. That gave me the confidence I needed and we decided to party on."

The gathering was a huge success.

Several years later, Dave had a torn tendon in his shoulder. He went to the doctor, who set Dave up for surgery.

"The day before surgery, I was feeling paranoid. I've never had surgery and wondered if I should get a second opinion," he says.

He called HEMPer Dr. Michelle Robin and she instantly made time to see him.

She reviewed the medical information and suggested Dave follow through with the procedure.

"She gave me the assurance I needed to go into the surgery," he says.

The information and connections Dave gained from HEMP continue to inform and improve his business practices and his life.

The Replay

THE SITUATION:

Dave Cacioppo and his partners were running a business without really understanding business basics.

- They were working hard yet never had any money left over.
- They didn't know how to read their financial statements.
- They were struggling to set up the right benefits packages.

THE SOLUTIONS:

- Analyze the bidding process to understand where you're losing money.
- Tone down the generous benefits package so it doesn't place a financial burden on the company.
- Develop hiring practices and select the best person for the job.

THE RESULTS:

Today, Dave is president/ CEO of Emfluence, a successful and growing full-service digital marketing agency.

- He's refined his financial and data analysis, setting up each area of service as its own profit center.
- He brings that focus on results to his clients, showing them how he's helping them make money.
- His continuing involvement in HEMP offers a way to share his own talents and assist other entrepreneurs.

Emily Voth and Indigo Wild:

CLEANING UP WITH FUN AND HEALTHY PRODUCTS

Hundreds of empty lip balm containers cluttered Emily Voth's kitchen counter, along with rosemary, basil, and mint from her garden. Steam from the double boiler fogged the window, and the aroma of warm beeswax and lavender filled the air. On the floor, Emily and her husband struggled with a giant mixer, trying to keep their new batch of soap from flying all over the room. It was eight o'clock on a Thursday night in 1996. Although she'd already spent a long day in her upstairs office, doing bookwork and making sales calls, for Emily the fun was just beginning.

"I was finally living my dream," she says.

Going from Drone to Dreamer

For nine years, she'd worked dutifully in corporate marketing and communications. But her job didn't motivate or excite her.

One day Emily was having lunch with her yoga teacher. "Is this what I'm supposed to be doing for the rest of my life?" Emily asked.

"Why don't you do something you're passionate about?" he suggested. "Why don't you turn a hobby into a business?"

His words inspired her. Emily loved her herb garden and she was interested in natural products, cosmetics, and skin care. She was also fascinated by aromatherapy, which was just becoming popular.

She began researching the ingredients of the expensive skin care products she bought at local department stores.

"I can do better than that," she thought.

She researched lip balm and soap recipes, analyzed the products currently on the market, and studied how various ingredients affected the skin.

Though she had no business background and little in savings, she decided to give her new idea a try. In 1996, when she was thirty years old, she quit her job and gave herself six months to make her dream of creating natural skin products a reality.

She used a favorite flower, wild indigo, as the inspiration for her company name and asked her architect husband to sketch up a logo and label. She created a batch of lip balms, bath salts, and facial creams and took her wares to a local organic farmers' market.

"We instantly sold out of everything," she says.

Making Soap While the Stars Shine

For eight months, Emily continued doing business from her home. Soon one bedroom was dedicated to shipping and receiving, one room was headquarters for sales and marketing, and another area was bulging with empty bottles, waiting to be filled. The

Charlie's angels: Lois Brayfield, Emily Voth, and Mary Lou Jacoby.

kitchen was production central. When she could barely squeeze through the house, she rented a space, moved her fledgling company, and began expanding her product line and growing her business.

Her husband helped and they often made soap late into the night, taking turns napping on the floor, cushioning themselves on discarded bubble wrap.

One night, she told her husband, "We must figure out a name for our soap."

After much brainstorming and a little wine, her husband said, "This sure is zum bar of soap."

Emily looked at him and said, "Zum bar! That's it! "And the Zum Bar and brand were born.

Part of Emily's joy in running her own business was the creative freedom.

"I could wear what I wanted, say what I wanted, listen to whatever music I liked, paint the walls bright colors, and I could bring my dogs to work," she says.

She poured in all her time and energy, creating new products and marketing to spas, gift shops, and specialty stores. Some days she spent hours trying to find retail markets, only to have one small gift shop sign on. Then she worked into the night, making products.

Despite the exhaustion and occasional frustration, Emily never considered giving up.

"Indigo Wild ignited something in me and that fire would not go out," she says.

In her first year of business, Whole Foods agreed to stock her products regionally. Soon, her products were nationally distributed. During this start-up period, Emily intuitively and organically created a bright, happy, caring workplace with fun-loving employees, along with some of their dogs. Every day, she and her staff stopped production and ate lunch together. The company became involved in various charities, focusing on breast cancer and dog rescue: areas of high interest to Emily and her employees.

In the fall of 2000, when her annual gross sales had reached $1 million, she joined HEMP, hoping to further grow and improve her business.

Learning That Help Is Everywhere

"I knew I needed guidance but I didn't even know what questions to ask," Emily says, of her initial HEMP experience. "I was open to all ideas. As I listened to other HEMPers, I realized there were many areas of possible improvement, including manufacturing, cash flow, and management."

Her mentor, Rick Krska, owner of the manufacturing company InkCycle, understood her business and offered invaluable insights and resources.

"He never gave me advice," Emily says. "But he did share his own stories and offered information that helped me make my own decisions."

Rick even asked his operations manager to evaluate Emily's production processes.

"Rick and his manager coached me on buying new equipment and guided me on what and where to buy," Emily says.

Rick Krska,
owner, InkCycle

Rick was like a business therapist. He listened deeply and helped Emily with manufacturing, money, and other issues. He also helped Emily learn the business side of managing employees.

"Discussing my company's problems with him really lowered my stress level," Emily says.

The HEMP community provided Emily with additional emotional support, practical advice, and a wealth of resources and connections.

"These entrepreneurs were staying up at night worrying about the same things I was stewing over," she says. "I really benefited by getting advice from several people before making my own decisions."

Selling Off the Shelves

One connection from a HEMPer proved to be a turning point for Indigo Wild.

A HEMP colleague suggested she meet Bob Sullivan, VP/chief sales and marketing officer at Boulevard Brewing Company.

During lunch, Emily described her business to Bob.

"Do you ever sell to grocery stores?" he asked.

"At that time, we were in Whole Foods and natural food stores," Emily says. "I had never thought of reaching out to conventional grocers."

She followed through on Bob's suggestion, and grocery stores have been a major source of growth ever since.

Her goal is to keep growing while enjoying the process.

"We don't have a big, complicated, cumbersome strategic plan," she says. "We just want to sell products that help people feel good and make a profit while having fun."

Continuing the Collaboration

Today, Emily serves as a HEMP Fellow. She still reaches out to other HEMPers and continues to learn from their experiences.

"I know I am not alone and that is a very comforting feeling," she says.

Jack Hayhow fits Emily Voth with her entrepreneurial boots as Tim Schaffer and Gabe Kaniger look on.

THE SITUATION:

Emily Voth was seeking information on ways to effectively grow her business.

- She had no business background and no peer group to consult.
- She had no particular expertise in manufacturing processes.

THE SOLUTION:

- Be open to all ideas.
- Consult several people before making a business decision.
- Connect with experts who understand equipment and manufacturing processes.

THE RESULTS:

Emily grew her business, and lived out her company mantra of selling products that help people feel good, while making a profit and having fun.

- Emily expanded her markets and grew her business nationally and internationally to more than three thousand accounts, including a dynamic web presence and an attractive mail-order catalog.
- Emily improved her manufacturing systems and her cash flow.
- Emily learned much from her peers, using those tips to improve aspects of her business.

Photo by Bruce Mathews.

Danny O'Neill and
the Rise of the Roasterie:

BREWING SUCCESS

"I've had my eye on you," the man said to Danny O'Neill. "I'm Barnett Helzberg, and I'd like to talk to you."

It was almost midnight on December 31, 1995. Danny was volunteering at a Kansas City Symphony event, serving coffee donated by his fledgling company, the Roasterie. Danny had never met Barnett but knew of his reputation as a stellar entrepreneur and businessman.

"You can talk to me anytime," Danny answered.

A few months later, Barnett placed a phone call that would transform Danny's life. Barnett invited Danny to join the newly created HEMP. Barnett told him Henry Bloch, founder of H&R Block, would be his mentor.

"It was fortuitous," Danny says. "My high school football coach used to tell us, 'If you position yourself for success, the probability of success is higher.'"

Climbing out of the Middle and onto the Top

Henry Bloch,
founder, H&R Block

Danny had worked hard to put himself in a position to succeed. Growing up in Denison, Iowa, in the middle of ten children, he was always the odd man out.

"I was very independent," he says. "I would never go with the group, sometimes on purpose."

In high school, he spent a year in Costa Rica as a foreign exchange student. During that time, he went coffee picking.

"I loved being with the farmers, and I loved the experience," Danny says.

That experience was ignited again after college. He worked in sales and marketing for Weyerhaeuser and spent a lot of time at the corporate headquarters in Seattle.

"I loved the coffee out there," Danny says.

He began to experiment, buying a hot-air popcorn popper and using it to roast coffee.

"I wanted to do something different, and the only idea I had was coffee," Danny says.

His friends mocked him, saying, "Good luck, making a living off that."

That friendly taunt inspired him.

Rediscovering His Passion

Though Danny was good at his job, he felt stifled. People were always trying to change him.

In 1991, he was transferred from Omaha to Kansas City. He had always planned to get an MBA, so he enrolled in the Rockhurst MBA Executive Fellows program. His entrepreneurial spirit grew on a 1992 Executive Fellows trip to Russia, where Danny joined business people and educators in facilitating workshops that taught the concepts of capitalism. Danny was inspired by the Russians' passion and enthusiasm for life.

"I used to be enthusiastic like that," Danny thought. Then he asked himself, "Why aren't I enthusiastic now?"

For Danny, that was an "aha" moment. He returned home, determined to do something different.

"Coffee once again came into my mind," he says. "I pushed it away because I didn't know enough about it. I couldn't imagine making a business out of it."

In June 1993, he took a year's leave of absence from his high-paying corporate job. He traveled the world, studying and researching coffee. He found an air roaster that produced a cleaner, smoother, mellower taste and had it delivered to his Brookside home. His new business, the Roasterie, was brewing.

Growing Gains: From Basement to Bedroom to Building

By November 1993, the Roasterie was incorporated. Danny made his first sale that December to an espresso cart in the University of Kansas Medical Center. As sales continued, the business moved from the basement and infiltrated the first floor of the house. Soon Danny had coffee sacks, packing materials, and a desk in his bedroom.

In March 1994, he hired his first employee. But he didn't really have enough money for payroll, so the man worked for free. In April, Danny hired additional help.

"You aren't making enough to pay me," his new employee informed Danny. "I'll work for free until you do."

For several months, Danny and his two-person staff worked without pay. In July 1994, he moved to a building in downtown Kansas City, Missouri. In August, the Roasterie was earning enough that Danny could make his payroll. He offered his two loyal workers a choice of back pay or stock. Both took stock, 5 percent for his original employee and 1 percent for his second worker.

As the business grew, Danny wanted to expand his thinking. He took a Fast-Trac course at the Kauffman Foundation. At one session, the facilitator described an entrepreneur:

"Thinks outside the box. Doesn't follow rules. Doesn't stand in straight lines."

"Wow," Danny thought, "that is me. I always had entrepreneurial instincts, but the system beat them out."

The qualities that had gotten Danny into trouble all his life were now characteristics to be proud of.

"I was thirty-five years old, and it was the first time I had been acknowledged and praised for being who I was," he says. "Plus, I was in a group of like-minded people."

The encouragement and acceptance he felt at Fast-Trac gave him the impetus he needed to steam ahead with his business.

Becoming the Perfect HEMP Prospect

In 1995, when Danny entered HEMP, he was an ideal mentee. He had an open mind and was eager to hear advice and follow through.

"Henry Bloch, a successful guy, wanted to help me," Danny says. "I was excited and I wanted to know what I could do better."

Right away, Henry and the HEMP team helped Danny think beyond the next sale.

"What is your potential?" they asked. "Ten years from today, what do you want to have accomplished?"

"I liked being around people who understood where I was and where I wanted to go," Danny says. "I had been in small business organizations and found too many people complaining about their problems. But the HEMP entrepreneurs were eager to crush obstacles, solve problems, and grow through innovation."

Christina Friederichs, Danny O'Neill, and Mindy Hamilton create the special HEMP Roasterie coffee blend.

Listening Creates a Million-Dollar Sale

At one of his early meetings with Henry, Danny carried in six big binders filled with accounting information.

Henry looked at him and said, "You don't want me to go through those do you?"

Instantly, Danny answered, "Of course not."

He wondered what they would do during their time together and he soon found out.

He talked, and Henry listened. Henry asked questions. Every so often, Henry offered a story, question, opinion, or advice.

Danny soaked in Henry's stories about serving in World War II. He listened raptly as Henry described his first small rented office on Main Street and eight years of knocking on doors and barely scraping by.

Danny was inspired by Henry's openness and vulnerability. He thought, "This is Henry Bloch, and he didn't have any money either."

One story was especially impactful. It was 1996, and Danny had been experimenting with producing two-ounce packages of coffee with special customized labels. The experiment was time-consuming and didn't seem to be bringing in a profit.

One day, Henry said, "Two years ago, I attended a Red Cross fund-raising dinner. They gave us small packages of your specially labeled coffee. I thought that was a nice gift."

Danny leaned forward. He thought of all the gifts Henry might have received in those two years. The fact that he remembered the packet of Red Cross coffee seemed significant and encouraged Danny to continue production.

A few months later, Danny was driving to a HEMP retreat when he received a phone call.

"Are you ready for your first million-dollar order?" a client asked.

She proceeded to order a million two-ounce coffee packets with a customized label that would market a new drug release.

Tom and Henry Bloch discuss Henry's life experiences with HEMPers.

"I was so grateful that I had really listened to Henry's comments," Danny says. "We bought a million dollars worth of equipment with that order and we are still using it today."

Taking One Cup at a Time

Henry's probing questions and cogent comments were another important component of the mentoring process.

"Have you thought about retail? That can be onerous, and you need a lot of money to do that," Henry said one day.

At the time, Danny thought opening a café wouldn't be such a big deal. Years later, when he finally decided to open a coffee shop, he thought about Henry's comments and realized how true they were.

"We had the same retail issues Henry talked about all those years ago, such as how to hire the right people," Danny says. In the midst of the retail chaos, he reflected on Henry's words and on a comment a restaurateur had made: "Danny, if you open the door to the public, the public might just come in."

Henry had encouraged Danny to enjoy the creative chaos of growing a business.

"Building a business is great fun," Henry told him.

"At the time I thought having a million dollars would be more fun," Danny admits. "But now I know Henry was right."

Learning from the Advisory Board

Danny's HEMP mentors and advisers encouraged him to create an advisory board.

"Choose folks whose only interest is your success," Barnett advised.

Within one week of hearing that advice, Danny began putting together his board. He invited a friend from college and a community business leader.

"I was naïve," he recalls. "I gave them no history or company background. I had no agenda. The first meeting was a disaster. My friend spent the hour talking about himself."

At a HEMP training session, Danny listened carefully to the discussion about whom to put on the board.

"Ask yourself, 'What does my company need?' Invite people who have the skills to deal with your current issues."

Danny tried again. But he made a key mistake.

"I didn't set term limits," he says. "To turn over the board, I had to fire people."

He soon remedied that error and designated one-year terms that were renewable.

"That way people could serve for a year and feel appreciated, even if I didn't renew," he says.

Danny stumbled into creating an effective board. At one meeting, he handed out thick packets of papers. A board member glanced through the ream and suggested, "Bullet points are better than paragraphs. You might want to hand these out several weeks in advance, so we are not sitting here reading."

Meeting by meeting, Danny learned from his board.

Translating Green Beans into Cash

The Roasterie was growing fast, but inventory was high, and Danny didn't have enough money to pay his bills. By June 1998, his financial situation seemed hopeless. He couldn't borrow any more money. The only way out of the hole was to sell part of his company. He agonized over the decision and came to the board meeting one night feeling glum and discouraged.

Barnett, Danny O'Neill, and Barnett's smarter, younger brother, Charley.

"We need money," he told the five board members. "There's no other way out. I have to sell 25 percent of the company."

One by one, each said, "I don't think you should sell any of the company."

"There's no other way," Danny said.

"There are other ways," one said.

"Show me because I've run out of ideas."

He instantly received this advice. "Call your suppliers and tell them you can't pay them until September, when you can turn the inventory into cash. Tell them, 'If you need to charge interest, go ahead.'"

Danny followed their advice and it worked. Only one vendor charged interest. By September, those pallets of green coffee beans translated into cash. Danny paid the bills and was grateful he had kept his company intact.

"I would have blown through any money from the sale," he says. "Then I would have had to go out into the market again to sell another portion of the company."

The next year, the Roasterie experienced the same kind of cash crunch. This time, Danny knew how to get through it.

Finding His Perfect Job

Some people start a company because they want to run it: Danny always felt he wanted to run from his company.

"I didn't want to do the day-to-day details," he says. "I wanted to find people who could do each job better than I could."

When he traveled, he entrusted his employees to run the business.

"Everything was usually better when I returned," he says.

Danny made two lists: work activities he loved and activities he loathed.

When he read the list of things he loathed, he realized it was the beginning of a job description for a CEO. He shared his list of dislikes with a board member, who said, "Those are all the things I enjoy doing."

In July 2010, Danny stepped down as CEO and his board member began the job.

"Once I stepped down, a load lifted off my shoulders," Danny says. "I now focus on the things I'm good at—being in charge of the mission, vision, strategy, and recruitment."

Getting Back a Hundred Times More

"Back in 1995, I didn't appreciate how lucky I was to be in the HEMP program," Danny says. "I didn't know the impact the program would have and the people I would meet as the result. The knowledge I received from HEMP continues to guide and impact my business decisions."

Danny applauds the program leaders for putting the right people together, then stepping back and letting the learning take place.

Danny continues to sift through the advice he received during his three years of formal mentoring. He also keeps growing through his association with HEMP participants and alumni. He has served as a mentor and continues his practice of actively giving back to his community.

Charitable giving has been key in helping his company gain visibility.

"Early on, I realized that giving to charities was a great way to get exposure for our little company," Danny says. "So, I basically just started donating to every charity that I saw in the paper."

Through those charitable contributions, he met leaders in all segments of the community, including Barnett Helzberg. He has updated the advice he received from the grade school nuns when he was growing up: "When you give back, you get back ten times more."

"I now believe, when you give, you get back a hundred times more," Danny says.

The Replay

THE SITUATION:

Danny O'Neill was growing fast and inventory outgrew cash reserves.
- He was behind in his bills.
- He was focused on the next sale, not on the big picture.
- He was overwhelmed and frustrated.
- He was ready to sell off 25 percent of his business to raise money.

THE SOLUTION:
- Put together an advisory board made up of people who have the skills the company needs and create term limits. Listen to their advice.
- Don't panic and don't sell any part of the company.
- Communicate honestly with vendors when you're in financial straits.
- Plan for such natural fluctuations in the future.

THE RESULTS:

Danny keeps his business intact during a period of precarious cash flow and continues to grow.
- Danny still owns 100 percent of the Roasterie.
- The business has grown steadily.
- Danny continues to listen to his advisory board.

Chuck and Ellene Hoffman stand on chairs to equalize heights with Danny O'Neill.

James Davis and Davis Safety Supply:

TAKING BUSINESS TO THE NEXT LEVEL

James Davis was ready to take his business to the next level. It was spring 2010 and Davis Safety Supply had been in business for eighteen years. Through hard work, determination, and unerring customer service, James had catapulted his original investment of $500 into a successful multidivisional cleaning and safety supply business worth millions. But James knew the company had more potential. He was expanding his product lines, including food services and an eco-division (Green Seal Certified and/or EPA approved Eco-friendly), and widening his delivery network. He planned to build a new warehouse. He envisioned an enterprise that grossed $600 million a year. But he didn't know how to take the next step.

When an employee mentioned HEMP, James signed up.

Learning from Ed Sullivan

James's penchant for entrepreneurship began when he was eleven years old. He started out simply enough, mowing a few lawns after school. By the time he was thirteen, he had hired other kids, expanded into more neighborhoods, and diversified into leaf raking and snow clearing. His work ethic was fierce, inspired by his father, who worked three jobs to provide for his family.

"I wanted to be successful and I had the confidence I could do anything," James says.

James was right to be confident. He had already taught himself to stop stuttering. When he was six, his stuttering was so pervasive that he failed first grade.

As the years passed, he vowed to overcome his speech difficulties. James typically rushed into speech, hoping to avoid getting trapped into stammering. One evening, he turned on the television and saw the Ed Sullivan variety show. He watched the array of entertainers on Ed Sullivan and noticed how slowly they spoke. Over the weeks, he studied the performers and emulated their speech patterns until he could control his own.

Using the $800 Springboard

James dropped out of high school and joined the army in 1974, when he was just sixteen.

"I wanted to go to war," he said. But he was too late for Vietnam. He served his time, then returned to Kansas City when he was nineteen. He started painting houses to make some money. One day, he noticed a little neighborhood general store that was for sale.

"I negotiated with the owner and bought the business for $800," James says.

He then began the all-consuming work of running the store. James paid attention to what his customers needed and wanted and he stocked it for them. He also handed out free candy to all kids who made straight A's.

"I gave credit, sold bus tokens, and offered nachos dipped in cheese," he says. "I was selling customer service. People like to deal with those who make them feel good, and I have a gift for that."

Within eight years, when the store was grossing $1.2 million a year, James sold the business and founded another.

Learning from Running Businesses

He started and sold five businesses before he founded Davis Safety Supply. His endeavors included a publishing company, hair care products, a limo and yacht luxury transportation service, a convenience store, and a restaurant just for kids, featuring nachos, hamburgers, and video games.

James had a gift for sales. While running the convenience store, he had the idea to start a safety company, featuring janitorial supplies, safety equipment, and food service supplies. During the second week of his fledging enterprise, he sold Procter and Gamble $19,000 worth of merchandise, making a profit of $11,000. "I decided to focus on developing Davis

Safety," James says.

Each entrepreneurial experience taught him something.

"Everything I know about customer service started in that first general store," James says. "The publishing business gave me the knowledge to put together our current catalogues."

Mentoring Magic

Dan McDougal,
founder,
Dredge America

In 2010, James felt his business had the potential to expand and diversify, but he didn't know how to make that happen.

His HEMP mentor, business veteran and former HEMP mentee, Dan McDougal, did.

"I want to make this business a great success," James told Dan.

"That takes a lot of work," Dan said.

"That's not a problem," James answered. James knew if he made too many mistakes, it would cost a lot of money. Through talking to Dan, he was able to learn from some of the errors Dan had made taking his business to the next level.

Though James had eighteen employees, he was a hands-on owner and fostered a mom-and-pop atmosphere. He wrote all the invoices himself, often waking up at 4 a.m. to get the job done. He pulled delivery orders to make sure they were correct. He did all the purchasing. His accounting help was well meaning but not professional. James worked constantly, making sure all the details were attended to.

Dan advised James to spend his time doing what he did best—getting new business. He steered James away from an expensive but unnecessary software program and steered him toward a professional accountant. He advised him to hire people to do some of the detail work.

"I was open to changing." James says. "I didn't have time to go to school. HEMP was and is my school."

Bob Brush,
Sam Meers, and
James Davis.

Attending the College of Experience

James was surprised by resources and information the other HEMP participants offered.

"The interaction between the peers has been positive," James says. "We're like an organization working together. I have always been on my own and never had anyone to talk to about business. I never knew other people had problems until I got into HEMP. Now, I can learn from other business folks."

The results have been heartening. His HEMP advisers urged him to hire more people and secure more customers before he started on his new building. He began developing a business plan so he could borrow money for the building.

"My mentor advised me to slow down and create the foundation for the next level of business," James says.

James is learning as fast as he can. He spends more time on selling and developing his business and is weaning himself away from micromanaging. Within five years, he envisions his business will be bringing in $75 million a year.

"HEMP is helping me transform the way I do business," James says. "These guys know what they're doing. I'm proud to be associated with these excellent business people and to learn from them. "

Combining Mom-and-Pop and HEMP

James still takes pride in the simple pleasures of a business well run.

"At the end of day, it's all about being happy," James says. "Every night, I ask my employees, 'Is everyone happy?' I'm really asking, 'Did every customer get everything they needed and do my employees feel good about their jobs?' When they answer me, 'Everyone is happy,' then I'm happy."

THE SITUATION:

James Davis wanted to take his business to the next level.

The Replay

THE SOLUTION:

- Listen to the advice of mentor and peers.
- Focus on what you do best.
- Create a business plan as a guide for expansion and growth.

THE RESULTS:

James starts moving to the next level of business success.

- Additional staff allows James to delegate some of the detail work.
- A professional on-staff accountant has cleaned up the accounting system.
- His HEMP team offers him an array of resources and information.

Photo by Bruce Mathews.

Michelle Robin and Your Wellness Connection:

GROWING THROUGH BECOMING THE UDM (ULTIMATE DECISION MAKER)

Michelle Robin's life was out of balance. She had worked hard building a thriving chiropractic and wellness practice. But she was starting to think that bigger wasn't necessarily better. She was constantly aware of her responsibilities and was the first to arrive at work and the last to leave. In addition to a full schedule of seeing clients, she also had to deal with staff and operational issues.

She wanted to become a better leader and a better business person. A friend told her about HEMP and she joined the program in 2003.

Meeting Memorable Mentors

Michelle grew up in a lower-middle-class household in Parsons, Kansas. When she was a high school freshman, she babysat for an entrepreneurial couple. Later, she worked in their bowling alley and in their pizza place.

"They taught me a lot about business," she says. "They were my first mentors and they also were like family."

When she was fifteen, Michelle sustained a sports injury and went to see Dr. Lakin, a local chiropractor.

"From him, I began learning about mind-body-spirit connection," she says.

She was fascinated by these new concepts and marveled at the body's capacity for healing. Dr. Lakin and his wife also mentored Michelle, helping her understand her own potential and encouraging her to live out her dreams.

Throughout high school, Michelle worked part-time in Dr. Lakin's office, doing x-rays, patient therapies, and phone calls. She continued to learn from his holistic approach to health, which included acupuncture and energy medicine.

When she attended chiropractic college, she encountered Richard Yennie, chiropractor and diplomate in acupuncture. She was taken with his knowledge and fascinated by his eastern philosophy and his integrated approach to healing. She attended his weekend training courses, but wanted to study directly with him.

"I will work for free," she told his assistant.

She was persistent in her desire to learn from him and finally, when she was twenty-three years old, she got the chance. During the two years she worked for him, he taught her about healing and also about practice management and building relationships with patients. Then he told her, "You're ready to go into business on your own."

Going from Bigger to Better

In 1992, Michelle opened her own chiropractic office. After seven years as a solo practitioner, she began adding associates and creating a wellness practice. She became increasingly visible in the community and built her brand. But as the business grew, her focus dissipated.

"In 2003, when I became part of HEMP, my organization included eight doctors with mediocre practices instead of four doctors with great practices," Michelle says.

She managed a total of thirty-five employees. The more people she employed, the harder she worked. She had a vision of where she wanted to go, but didn't know how to get there.

Her HEMP mentor Bill Reisler, managing partner of Consumer Growth Partners, helped her get clear on her direction.

Bill was an excellent sounding board, offering feedback on various aspects of the business.

"I love mentoring and guiding people, but I was doing that to the detriment of my own health and finances," Michelle says. "I was too enmeshed in the details of the business and Bill helped me see that."

Bill Reisler,
*managing partner,
Consumer Growth
Partners*

With Bill's guidance, she stopped being over-accommodating and began holding her staff more accountable. She put additional financial procedures in place and created a compensation strategy for her staff. She went electronic with scheduling and billing. These changes improved the business's efficiency and allowed her to reduce her staff.

Most importantly, she worked on understanding what she really loved doing.

"I'm in a room six hours a day, not running my business, just caring about people," she says. "HEMP helped me realize I love doing that and it's OK."

In 2005, she changed the name of her business to reflect her intention to connect each client with his or her own wellness: Robin Chiropractic & Acupuncture Center officially became Your Wellness Connection.

Becoming the UDM

During the mentoring program, Michelle often heard Bill and other HEMPers talk about the importance of being the company's UDM, the Ultimate Decision Maker. As the UDM, you have control of your schedule.

Four years after the formal HEMP training, Michelle took control of her own schedule and shortened her business hours.

"This was a transformative decision," Michelle says. "I added a couple of extra hours to my day, to spend time with my family, work out or do other things I enjoy. I am now more peaceful. My staff was also delighted with the change."

She continues to learn from HEMP as a Fellow and as a member of the Mentee Committee.

"Being part of HEMP allows me to be my best self," she says.

Michelle Robin and Dan Nilsen enjoy HEMPing at an event.

The Replay

THE SITUATION:

Michelle Robin had a thriving business but an unbalanced life; she was working too much and too hard.

- The more employees she had, the harder she worked.
- She wanted to become a better business person.
- She wanted to live out her goals but didn't have a clear plan or path.

THE SOLUTION:

- Add in processes and procedures to streamline operations.
- Automate billing and scheduling, therefore reducing staff and increasing efficiency.
- Hold people accountable and don't over-accommodate.
- Do what you love.

THE RESULTS:

Michelle is now happier and more balanced.

- She's become the UDM and now controls her own schedule.
- She's focusing on patient healing and interaction, which she loves.
- She's reduced her staff for a more peaceful and focused business.

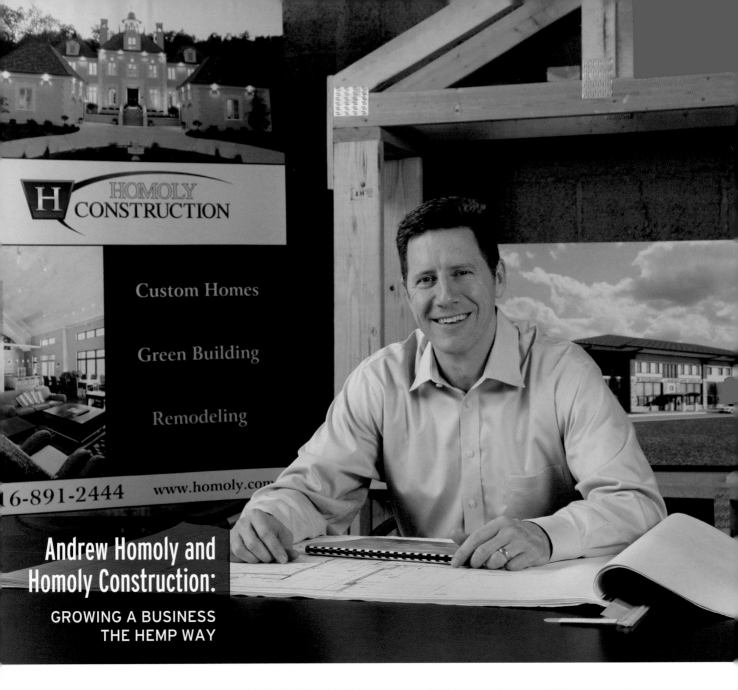

Andrew Homoly and Homoly Construction:

GROWING A BUSINESS THE HEMP WAY

Andrew Homoly had a big idea that was outside the normal scope of his construction business. He wanted to present this bold idea to Warren Buffett.

"You should contact Barnett Helzberg," a business acquaintance advised. "He knows Warren."

"Can you introduce me?" Andrew asked.

"No. I won't introduce you. Barnett will appreciate it if you can figure out how to meet him on your own."

Andrew returned to his office and Googled Barnett. HEMP came up.

"If my company is accepted into HEMP, I will meet Barnett," Andrew thought.

Just Muscling Along

That spring of 2006, Andrew's business, Homoly Construction, which specialized in custom homes and commercial construction, was eight years old. The business was grossing about $1.5 million in annual sales and had five employees.

"We were in business, but everything was a battle," Andrew recalls. "We were muscling along on sheer willpower, dedication, and hard work."

Andrew didn't know how to expand the business. He figured if he just worked hard, it would all come together.

"I figured the success would just come naturally, but hard work alone was not getting it done," he says.

He wondered if HEMP could help. He submitted an application and received a site visit.

"Sure enough, Barnett came along on that visit," Andrew says. He showed Barnett the large project he had in mind. Barnett was impressed with Andrew's entrepreneurial initiative and Andrew was accepted into the program.

Listening to the Sawdust in his Blood

"Get a good education and get the hell out of the construction business!" That was the advice Andrew's father gave him, as he trained Andrew and his brother in the trade that his father had trained him in. Andrew and his brother worked every summer, pouring concrete, plumbing, wiring, building homes, and helping their father in his business.

"Dad gave us the most difficult jobs," Andrew says. "He wanted us to know that building was grueling work."

Andrew listened to his father's advice and received a civil engineering degree from the University of Illinois. In 1992, he took a job with Exxon, planning to build a career with them. But four years into his climb up the corporate staircase, he had a defining life moment.

"I realized that I loved to build things," he says. "I had sawdust in the blood."

He had never thought about being an entrepreneur, but he didn't want to be an executive in a big company. He started asking himself what he wanted to do with his life and decided he wanted to start a construction company. He was so ready to get on with his dream he didn't even stay the extra six months it took to become vested.

His wife's family lived in Kansas City and Andrew's research showed the area was an open market for a new construction business. In 1996, he and his family moved to the Kansas City area. After a year working for a small civil engineering firm, getting to know the market, building a house or two, and working on his grand plan, he began Homoly Construction.

From Creating a Job to Building a Company

That fall of 2006, as he began HEMP, Andrew was ready to expand and grow his business.

"If you want to grow, you need to treat this more like a company," Andrew's mentor, Ted Murray, CEO of Colliers International Kansas City, said on their initial visit.

First, Andrew got his finances in order. His philosophy had been, "If there's money in

Ted Murray,
CEO Colliers International Kansas City

the checking account, things are good. If not, things are bad." He wasn't budgeting or creating monthly statements.

While he was working with Ted to get his finances in order, Barnett recommended two books that really got him thinking: *The E-Myth* by Michael Gerber and *Good to Great* by Jim Collins.

"After reading them, I realized I had created a job for myself, but I hadn't created a company," he says.

With Ted's guidance, he created a business plan.

"My former plan was, 'Get work, do work,'" Andrew says.

Part of the new plan included making enough steady income to hire an estimator and a marketing director.

Ted advised him to give up his home office and move to a more professional setting. Andrew resisted. Then one day, one of Andrew's most important clients dropped by his "office" unannounced. The man rang the door bell and Andrew answered, with his three-year-old and a barking dog close behind.

"I saw the skeptical look in his eye as he handed over the plans," Andrew says.

After the client left, Andrew said to his wife, "It's time to get an office."

Several months later, they moved to a dedicated office space in Kansas City, Missouri.

"Our credibility was instantly improved," Andrew says. "That office space put us in the ball game for bigger projects."

Thinking Big by Doing the Little Things

In addition to being more professional, Ted and HEMP encouraged Andrew to set goals and really work on the business, instead of grinding away in the field all day.

Andrew listened intently to Ted's advice and followed through on his suggestions. He also attended HEMP events, including Lunch with the Big Guy (LWTBG), retreats and educational programs.

"Every time I went to LWTBG, I got ideas," he says.

These ideas in areas such as marketing, IT, and client management, added up to make the business better.

Ted also suggested Andrew find a peer industry group. Andrew discovered the Builder 20 Club, a group of noncompeting custom home builders from across the country who met semiannually to share best practices. From them, he learned about benchmarking financial and other data against the top builders in the country. He implemented several best practices and continues to learn from his group.

"We kept fine-tuning the business, "Andrew says. "During our three years in HEMP, our company grew 330 percent."

In 2009, Homoly Construction was named the fifth fastest growing company in Kansas City. This was in a period of economic downturn when the construction industry was being pummeled.

"I owe our growth to HEMP," Andrew says.

Going to the Next Level

Today, Andrew is constantly evaluating his next steps. He is thinking strategically and looking to the future.

"We are a $6.5 million company," he says. "We're now bidding on a job that could make us a $12 to $15 million company."

Several years ago, his father and brother joined him as project managers. His wife works part-time in the office. He has an accountant, lawyer, and financial planner. Even though he has graduated from HEMP and is a Fellow, he and his mentor still meet every month. He's constantly reaching out for new ideas and enjoys being on the leading edge of a rapidly changing industry.

The big idea that initially led him to HEMP is still in the works. But Andrew's been so busy with his successful company and family he hasn't had time to devote himself to the project.

Andrew enjoys meeting with people who are starting businesses. He wants to share some of the information he has learned from HEMP.

"I did it the hard way for eight years without much guidance," he says. "If only I could have been part of HEMP earlier, who knows where I would be now."

The Replay

THE SITUATION:

Andrew Homoly was working hard but didn't know how to grow his business.

- He was immersed in the daily grind and wasn't engaged in big-picture thinking.
- He wasn't attuned to his financial status.
- His home office detracted from his professionalism.

THE SOLUTION:

- Create a budget and thorough monthly financials.
- Reach out to peer groups to better understand industry standards and best practices.
- Rent office space to enhance the company's brand and professionalism.

THE RESULTS:

By following HEMP advice and using industry standards, Andrew grows more than 300 percent within three years.

- Revenues climb to $6.5 million.
- He is named the fifth-fastest-growing business in Kansas City.
- He's a champion of HEMP and helps others who are thinking of starting their own businesses.

Leanne Cofield and Visage, Inc.:
A QUICK COURSE IN BUSINESS AND PROMOTIONS

"I'm being deployed to Bosnia," Leanne Cofield's employer told her. "I'm either going to shut down the company or you can buy it."

"I want to buy it," Leanne said.

That spring of 2002 was a busy time for thirty-four-year-old Leanne. She had a new baby and had only worked at Visage, Inc. for one year. As the company's one full-time employee, she sold promotional marketing items, such as customized mugs, pens, and T-shirts. She had never been an entrepreneur, though she'd often thought about running her own business. She was experienced in sales, having worked as a retail manager and buyer for Worth Harley-Davidson, before moving into the field of promotional marketing.

"I loved sales," Leanne says. "But I wanted to do more with my life. When the opportunity to buy the business popped up, I took it."

Learning the New

Four months later, she had a new business, which she initially operated out of her home. At the time of purchase, Visage, Inc. was grossing around $650,000 a year. Leanne first concentrated on surviving. She had no formal training, no entrepreneurial experience, and no guidance.

"The business completely consumed me," she says. "It wasn't about growth and processes; it was about taking care of the customers and keeping my head above water."

For the first year, Leanne did the bulk of the selling. Because she was a new business owner working globally, her vendors required prepayment via credit card. But instead of paying off her credit cards every month, she spent her money in other ways. The credit card debt rose and by the time she paid the accumulated interest, she was losing money.

"I thought if my receivables were high or if I had cash in the bank, I could spend that money instead of paying off my debt," she says. "I was so buried in keeping up with the customers that I didn't really deal with the financial aspects of the company."

Though she had a line of credit, she was scared to use it. She thought borrowing on her credit line was worse than credit-card debt.

After a year of working from home, she moved into a small office space. Her mother worked part-time, helping with administrative tasks. Leanne hired two part-time sales people who worked from their homes. Then she began experiencing quality control issues that she didn't know how to solve.

"I had no idea if I was doing anything right," she says. "I'd never developed a business plan. I didn't have written procedures. I didn't understand the balance sheet. And I was working so hard I didn't have time to reach out to people."

Leanne signed up for leadership training programs but didn't get the help she needed.

"I was looking for a mentor, someone I could bounce around ideas with. But I didn't know how to find him or her," Leanne says.

Meanwhile, during the 2008 recession, Leanne's revenues plummeted. A major customer, representing 40 percent of her business, drastically cut his promotional budget. Another large customer also severely curtailed promotional spending. Suddenly, Leanne was struggling to survive.

Building the Business

"I want to build my business. And I want to be able to walk into any business and know how to run it." In 2009, when she joined HEMP, Leanne shared those goals with her mentor Dick Benner, project manager and board director of Executive Service Corp. of Greater Kansas City.

Leanne and Dick began meeting weekly. He looked at her books and explained the financials. He suggested areas that they should focus on fixing.

Her initial focus included reducing debt, putting procedures in place, improving quality control, and analyzing her own strengths and weaknesses.

"HEMP encouraged me to put my worst foot forward and I did," she says. "It was embarrassing to admit I didn't understand my financial statements. But I didn't know enough to fake it. I was embarrassed for a week and then I got over it."

With Dick's guidance, they went through the financials line by line and took out all the fluff.

"I could see the progress almost immediately," Leanne says. "Within the first year, I was almost debt-free."

Dick Benner,
retired corporate officer,
Avon Products

Within two years, she had gotten rid of all the credit cards.

Dick also advised her to go to her landlord and renegotiate the rent.

"Tell him that the economy is tough and you need some help."

She followed his advice and got her rent reduced for a period of time.

They tackled the quality control issues.

"What are your procedures?" Dick asked her.

She told him.

"Does everyone follow these procedures?"

She had to admit that they did not.

"I wasn't a stickler on procedures and systems. I believed that people could take their own path in getting things done," Leanne says. "But that doesn't work when you're running a business."

She brought in her staff and they talked through the ordering and quality control processes. With Dick's assistance, she and her staff developed a seamless multistep system for quotes, orders, deliveries, and sign-offs.

Promoting by Looking Within

Dick helped Leanne become aware of her own behavior.

"I learned I wasn't giving people enough positive feedback," she says. "I assumed they knew they were doing a great job."

She became more intentional with her communications, praising people and acknowledging accomplishments in meetings. Sometimes she bought small gifts for those who were doing outstanding work.

She also began to let go of some control.

She hired more staff, including a manager to work with her two new administrative people, who specialized in handling quoting and the order/production process. She brought in a sales manager so she was no longer mired in hiring and training the sales force.

"I realized how far I had evolved when I was out of town for a week and I didn't call into the office once," she says.

One of her customers told her, "You have a well-oiled machine."

Leanne was appreciative of her smoothly running business. Yet, she also realized, "The minute I think I know everything, I'm doomed."

Seeing a Visage of the Future

Now that she has debt reduced, processes in place, and a management team, Leanne's life has become much richer.

"I plan to build the business and sell within ten years," she says.

She has a new office in Parkville, Missouri, and works more on the business itself, focusing on building a new website, revamping her brand, and analyzing ways to expand.

"I hope to have five new sales people in the near future," she says.

With her sales team, she's creating a thorough training program for sales personnel. She's also exploring ways to even out cash flow, working to get contracts as a preferred vendor for large companies who consistently do promotional events. In her industry, contracts are an important step. Her mentor and sales team are working with her on that complicated process.

Leanne's quick course in small business has served her well. In 2009, she was barely at $1 million in sales. In 2011, her goal was $2 million in sales.

"We have made astonishing progress," Leanne says. "We've developed a larger and more diverse client base and now have the foundation to support our sales growth."

Thanks to the help and encouragement of Dick and other HEMPers, Leanne has met her initial goals. Her business is growing and she understands her financial situation. She feels like she can walk into any small business and understand how to run it.

Additionally, she no longer feels isolated.

"I went from being stranded on a desert island to becoming part of this welcoming entrepreneurial community," she says. "My company is thriving and my job is easier and more fun than it's ever been."

The Replay

THE SITUATION:

Leanne Cofield needed guidance, knowledge, and a way out of her debt.

- Her revenues plummeted, because of an economic recession and overreliance on two major customers.
- Debts mounted, due to using credit cards to operate the business.
- Quality-control issues plagued her.
- She didn't understand the financial aspects of her business.

THE SOLUTION:

- Analyze every expense and look for ways to cut out unnecessary costs.
- Learn to read and consistently review financial data.
- Broaden and diversify the customer base.
- Add in systems and procedures.
- Relinquish control and learn to delegate to responsible employees.

THE RESULTS:

Leanne grows her business through working on big-picture issues.

- Revenues increased by 45 percent in two years.
- She increased her employee base, adding in a sales manager and administrative manager.
- She let go of the daily details and concentrates on building visibility, brand, reputation, and revenues.

CHAPTER 10

BECOMING A NONPROFIT ENTREPRENEUR

MS™

National Multiple Sclerosis Society

Kay Julian
and the National Multiple Sclerosis Society Mid America Chapter:
ENGAGING THE BOARD

Kay Julian is a different kind of entrepreneur. She hasn't financed her business with her own money, but she faces many of the issues any entrepreneur must confront. As president of the National Multiple Sclerosis Society, Mid America Chapter, she runs an autonomous nonprofit, charged with raising money, understanding and meeting client and community needs, and partnering with other organizations to deliver services. She faces staffing and budgetary challenges. Often, she faces them alone.

"As the CEO, I can't just gush out every worry to the board or the staff," she says. "Before I joined HEMP, I had been searching for a mentor and community of peers. I wanted more people I could learn from."

Finding Her People

Kay found that community and the mentoring she wanted in HEMP.

It was 2004. A friend had been through HEMP and emphasized how much it had helped her business. She recommended Kay and within a year, Kay represented one of the first nonprofits to be part of the program. Kay had experience in the nonprofit world and had been president of the Mid America Chapter of the National MS Society for eleven years. She was ready to deepen her leadership skills and to take the organization to the next level.

"I am a huge believer in never staying still," she says. "I believe in stretching myself and being exposed to a variety of people, experiences, and learning."

She was gratified to have as her mentor, Bill Eddy, dean emeritus of the Bloch School at UMKC, and a veteran in nonprofit management.

"He understood the nonprofit culture and constituents," she says.

Permission to Be Vulnerable

Kay saw the mentoring relationship as a safe place to openly show her uncertainties, discuss her concerns, and seek guidance and growth.

"What a relief to say to Bill, 'I'm not sure I handled this well,' and then talk through the situation in detail," she says. "Bill had no judgment toward me. He asked the right questions and probed to get at the core of the issue."

The permission to be vulnerable helped Kay keep her perspective and her sanity through some challenging times.

"I had a safety valve and could constructively discuss issues with someone who had specific knowledge of what I was working through," she says.

Her mentor's professional and focused feedback helped Kay clarify her own thinking and fine-tune her decision-making.

Bill Eddy,
dean emeritus,
UMKC Bloch School
of Business

Getting the Board on Board

Kay was at a crossroads: She had a strong board that she wanted to make even stronger so the organization could reach its bold goals. Bill guided her with a series of thought-provoking questions, including, "How do we more fully engage board members? How do we add a financial commitment as an integral part of board service? How do we communicate this new commitment and get the current leadership to own it? How do we add in behavioral and action-oriented commitments?"

"We wanted people to attend meetings and be invested in our mission," Kay says. "Our board was already giving, but we wanted to create a more formal expectation tied to the support of our new organizational goals."

Bill guided Kay through analyzing the status of the current board. Then they strategized ways she could:

- Share and create mutual goals.

- Introduce the concept of increased commitment.

- Track the results.

- Share the results in a way that built partnerships.

Kay's chapter continues to benefit from the results of that strategic and analytical process.

"Today, we have a fully engaged and invested board," she says.

She personally updates board members quarterly, giving them an overview of their financial contributions and commitments.

"These communications are a great way to stay in touch," Kay says.

At board meetings, the chair thanks individual members for their specific volunteer contributions. Kay also shares the summary of board accomplishments at the meetings.

"Our work is about raising money, of course," Kay says. "But it's also about getting a share of someone's heart."

Growing into a Stronger Leader

Kay built on her knowledge base by connecting with her HEMP peers and attending educational HEMP retreats. At one session, the presenter demonstrated a tool that helped break down long-term and short-term personal goals.

"I constantly use this technique," Kay says. "This tool helps me set my intentions and focus on the smaller steps necessary to achieve them."

She appreciated the diversity of the businesses represented at HEMP.

"If you're passionate about being a leader and care about being successful, it doesn't matter if you're an entrepreneur or a nonprofit leader," she believes. "I grew from being around creative, energetic people who were invested in what they're doing, and passionate about their cause or business."

At the end of the process, Kay was a better and more confident leader with a stronger and more engaged organization.

THE SITUATION:

Kay Julian wanted to build a more engaged and financially committed board.

- The board was functioning well, but there was no formal contribution component.
- She wanted the board more fully engaged and involved in supporting the organization's bold new goals.

THE SOLUTION:

- Understand the current status quo.
- Create a process for redefining board commitment and set goals.
- Design a communication that creates a sense of excitement and engagement.
- Stay in touch with the board.

THE RESULTS:

Kay strategically designs ways to increase the board's involvement and financial commitment.

- All board members are contributing financially.
- Board members are more engaged and active, which positively impacts the entire organization.

Gina Pacumbaba-Watson celebrates her success.

Bush Helzberg shows Jay Tomlinson cheating techniques.

Al Capone and girlfriend.

Jeff Cates, Mark Spears, Bob Bennett, and Bob Nixon display their enthusiasm for HEMP.

HEMP culture includes serious immersion in yellow mustard.

HEMP beauty pageant winners, Gina Stuelke and Melody Warren.

Harvey Thomas and Ellene Hoffman roar with laughter.

Jay Beller shows off his Build a Bear t-shirt during Maxine Clark's team building exercise.

Dawn Eddy Rashid rolls her usual 7.

Barnett Helzberg and Christina Friederichs enjoy a wonderful gathering hosted by Dan and Renee McDougal.

PART 3

CREATING A CULTURE OF CONNECTION

Chuck Hoffman pays serious attention during a HEMP board meeting.

Ray Pitman and Kathy Koehler need more cowbell!

Supermodel Shirley Bush Helzberg with Bob Epsten.

Jack and Lois Sladkey at Celebrate HEMP.

Kansas City's top auctioneer, Jeff Cates, demonstrates his skills.

Dan McDougal and Don Proffer share enjoyment of a mentoring event.

Mike O'Malley, Paul and Shannah Kushnir, and Judy Minor witness Al Capone's hot roll.

CHAPTER 11

MATCHMAKING

Typically, mentee/mentor relationships occur by accident, through networking, business, or social organizations. HEMP always faces the challenge of successfully matching a mentor with a mentee.

Christina Friederichs,
HEMP managing director

The Selection Process

The HEMP team attracts mentees by consulting with the Chamber of Commerce, reviewing Top Ten lists, sending letters to promising entrepreneurs, and networking.

"Each year we welcome ten to fifteen new mentees into the three-year program," says Christina Friederichs, managing director, HEMP. "Matching is a challenge and we're always fine-tuning the process." Here is the current selection process:

- Mentees fill out applications.
- The HEMP managing director does background and reference checking.
- The Mentee Selection Committee reviews applications and determines who qualifies for a site visit.

The traveling squad visit Stuart Jackson at AnalyzeDirect.

- In August, a HEMP team tours the business and interviews the entrepreneur.
- Decisions are made and applicants are informed by phone calls and congratulatory letters.

The Match-up

- The new mentees attend orientation in September. Before they are matched, they are connected with a mentee graduate, who introduces them to mentors and other HEMPers.
- Once the mentees receive informational packets describing the available mentors, they're encouraged to meet and connect with those who interest them. They're also encouraged to attend various HEMP educational and networking events. During this period they're learning about HEMP and familiarizing themselves with the mentors.
- Mentees attend a speed-matching event, where they pick their top three potential mentors.
- At the end of the evening, mentees list their prioritized choices. Mentors also write down their prioritized choices.
- The Mentee Selection Committee makes matches based on the ranked order and on site visit recommendations.

Finding a Match

The HEMP team created a list to help facilitate the matching process.
This list also works well for an individual entrepreneur seeking his or her match.

Deborah Young,
principal,
Organizational
& Management
Consulting

- Know what you want. For mentees, this means listing goals and issues they need help with. For mentors, this means writing down what they want from the mentoring experience.
- Learn about each other. Read background materials. Get together to talk.
- Go beyond the obvious. Think of your perfect mentor, then think of the opposite.
- Know yourself and your openness to listening to others.
- Be prepared to talk honestly. The more you can share, the more beneficial your relationship will be.

"Often, we're attracted to someone who is like us, with the same style, same sense of humor and similar interests," says Deborah Young, PhD, principal, Organizational & Management Consulting. "It's more effective to select a mentor who has some strengths you don't have."

Here are some of the key learnings from HEMP's evolution.

DO select mentees who:

- Run a financially stable business.
- Want to expand and improve their business.
- Get along with others and will participate in the group.

- Will contribute and give back to the group and the community.
- Pass all the selection criteria.
- Will sign the written contract that allows you to do background checks and terminate the relationship if needed.

When selecting mentees, DON'T:

- Pick two people from the same company.
- Select someone who's not the ultimate decision-maker.
- Include someone who's a loner and doesn't want to listen and learn.
- Select friends or others who don't meet the criteria.

DO pick mentors who:

- Have time and patience. This may mean reaching out to retired business professionals or entrepreneurs whose businesses are stable and running.
- Are humble and open to learning.
- Have experience with both success and challenges.

When selecting mentors, DON'T:

- Select non-listeners.
- Select egomaniacs.
- Select people "who never have made a mistake."
- Select people without a generous heart.

Monitoring Matches

Some meetings begin with a connective question such as, "What is one of your top business issues?" These conversations encourage mentees and mentors to:

- "Put your worst foot forward" and talk about mistakes and mishaps.
- Listen without judgment.
- Share resources and information.
- Look for ways to support and boost each participant.

After every meeting, both mentee and mentor are invited to go online and answer a survey with questions such as:

- Do you feel like you and your mentor are working towards the same goals?
- Are you getting the support you need?

Tracking mentee/mentor progress is an integral part of the managing director's job.

"I call and check in with each mentee quarterly," says Christina. "I personally meet with them at the end of each year."

Quarterly Conversations

The extra monthly tracking helps, sometimes. Some mentees give one-word answers. Some don't fill out the forms; they are independent entrepreneurs, after all. That's why the quarterly phone call is so important. During the conversation, Christina asks specifically about challenges. She often asks the "three magic questions":

- What are we doing that you like?
- What are we doing that you don't like?
- What are we not doing that you would like?

"These discussions help me develop relationships with the mentees, so I can serve as a resource," Christina says. "I also encourage them to connect with their peers."

Occasionally a member of the Mentee Selection Committee also follows up with the mentor or mentees.

"It helps to have an extra person involved," Christina says.

Anniversary Talks

During her yearly meeting, Christina talks extensively with each mentee, discussing issues such as:

- Are we doing a good job?
- Are the events and programs working?
- How are things going with your mentor?
- What would make the relationship better?

For the final graduation meeting, Christina discusses company growth in terms of revenue and employees. She asks the entrepreneurs to describe the successes and failures over the three years and the lessons learned.

"I want to know what they've learned from the program so we can be more effective," she says.

What to Do When the Match Doesn't Ignite

A good central office person is key to consistently interacting with mentors and mentees.

A simple phone call can often give perspective or iron out a difficulty in the mentor/mentee relationship.

"The board isn't there every day," Bill Eddy says. "You need a manager who can deal with issues as they come up."

When relationship challenges arise, here are some options:

- The manager of the program can discuss the issues with the mentee, asking probing questions and finding out if there are ways to improve or mend the relationship.
- She can suggest a trial period, with new guidelines for the mentoring relationship.
- If the mentoring is simply not working, she can assist in ending the relationship and finding a new mentor.

Bill Eddy,
dean emeritus,
UMKC Bloch School
of Business

CHAPTER 12

CREATING ADVISORY BOARDS

Five people sit around the table, reviewing the company's financial statements.

"Why are you carrying so much inventory?" one of the members asks.

"I'm saving by buying in bulk," the entrepreneur responds.

"Have you analyzed the cost of tying up so much money and so many resources?" There's a silence.

"No, I really haven't," the entrepreneur says.

"It looks like you're relying on one carrier for distribution," another board member says. "Is that wise?"

At the end of the session, the entrepreneur is left with a list of things to analyze and consider, challenging the procedures he's been using for years. Part of him feels resistant—after all, he's gotten this far. Another part feels relieved—he's getting feedback from successful business leaders who have been through similar growing periods. He knows he is going to benefit from his advisory board.

Alice and Ted Cohn – treasured HEMP resources.

Anchoring Through Advisory Boards

Entrepreneurs often feel alone. Having a mentor and being part of the HEMP community changes that sense of isolation. Working with an advisory board creates an additional sounding board and safety net.

Ted Cohn, consultant, friend of HEMP, and author of *Management Smarts*, wrote this about advisory boards: "A board is a forum where the CEO and perhaps a few key managers can test their assumptions, have a place to resolve their differences, get opinions and ideas from people with different backgrounds, and become more effective by being accountable on a regular basis to a group of peers."

HEMP recommends mentees create their own advisory boards. When putting together a board, Cohn advises these considerations:

- Choose CEOs who are independent and not related to or employed by the entrepreneur.
- Select people who are not afraid to speak frankly.
- Seek active CEOs from large successful firms. Since the entrepreneur is growing his firm, a CEO with experience along these lines is most helpful.
- Look for generalists, not specialists. For expertise in a certain area, hire a consultant.

- Choose CEOs from other industries. They can challenge industry assumptions and give the entrepreneur new angles on old problems.
- Set up an annual evaluation, where the CEO gives the board feedback, letting them know how they can be more helpful. The board should give the CEO feedback as well.

Making Meetings Matter

Many HEMPers have benefited from advisory boards. Their tips include:

- Schedule quarterly meetings.
- Don't use friends or family.
- Don't use anyone who has a conflict of interest such as your banker, lawyer, accountant, or brother-in-law.
- Have a clear agenda for each meeting and let board members know the agenda well in advance, so they can prepare.
- Keep the board small, between three to five people.
- Create term limits. If a board member isn't working, term limits allow for a natural rotation.

DOES IT HELP MENTEES?

HEMP's goal summarized.

STEERING HEMP TOWARD CHANGE

Lirel Holt,
CEO, U, Inc.,

When Lirel Holt, CEO, U, Inc., became president of HEMP in 2007, the organization began to change its internal practices.

"It was a fascinating time. We had the accumulated knowledge of great mentors, mentees, and HEMP staff," Lirel says. "I wanted to make sure we captured the wealth of information, including how Barnett started HEMP, how the organization was structured, and the mentoring methods."

Lirel was a founding mentor of HEMP and had worked with many entrepreneurs both through HEMP and other businesses. He knew firsthand the power of business mentoring.

"I wanted to preserve the best of HEMP for the future," he says.

Lirel was the perfect person to do that.

From Automotive to Automated Success

During the early 1970s, Lirel worked his way through the University of Missouri-Kansas City restoring exotic cars. Borrowing money from his father, he would buy a rusty exotic car, restore it, sell it, repay his father, and use the profits to fund his college tuition.

"My dad gave me a good working knowledge of cars and let me use our garage," Lirel says. "I read every motor and hot rod magazine. I worked retail at an area auto parts store and began to understand how business, cars, and customers came together."

Throughout college and after graduation in 1973, word spread that Lirel could handle exotic motors, classic cars, and national-level restoration. Celebrity vehicles began to arrive, including John Lennon's Rolls Royce, the king of Bahrain's Rolls Royce Corniche convertible, and the prince of Saudi Arabia's Porsche (matched to the prince's eye color).

After graduation, Lirel's love for cars grew into a full-blown business. He bought property, built a facility, and grew the company to twenty-five employees.

Having taken computer programming in college, he began to automate his financial systems and repair estimates. But the going was slow and frustrating, so Lirel joined forces with a Silicon Valley software startup undertaking a similar venture. He contributed to the software development and test marketed the management system in his own facility. Within a year, 3M Company acquired the software company. The division head asked Lirel if he would write and teach a multiday business workshop focused on how small to medium companies could use computer technology to manage, market, and handle accounting requirements. Lirel accepted the challenge.

During the week, Lirel ran his automotive business. But each Friday morning, he jumped on an airplane and flew to New York or Honolulu or Toronto, where 3M had seventy-five to one hundred automotive business owners and managers waiting to learn how automation, systems, and computers could help them.

3M expanded the program to encompass the entire U.S. and Canada and asked Lirel to work full time marketing and managing the program. Lirel sold his business and focused on the program, which grew from 50 to 175 workshops a year.

But six years later, Lirel was road-weary and started looking for other business ventures. In 1989 he discovered an opportunity in the collision segment of the automotive industry. He founded CARSTAR, a network of franchised and company-owned collision repair shops.

The attorney he consulted said, "Mr. Holt, I'll take your money to form the company, but it won't work."

Eight years later, when Lirel sold controlling interest in CARSTAR, it was the largest collision repair franchise in the world, with 350 stores in North America. The franchises and company stores repaired more than 175,000 cars a year, generating combined annual revenues of over $375 million. For his innovative work in the industry, Lirel was named an Ernst and Young Entrepreneur of the Year, and chosen as one of the automotive industry's Top Twenty-five Most Influential Leaders of the 20th Century in collision repair.

After leaving CARSTAR, Lirel and his sons started U, Inc., an online education company. "We exist to serve and we work for U!" was their motto. U, Inc. now provides online training to more than eighteen thousand companies, cities, counties, and organizations (including HEMP).

Changing a Changing Organization

From his franchise background, Lirel knew that a system wasn't official until it existed in writing. He was determined to document the HEMP systems and make the information available online. He based his approach on the book *The E-Myth* and brought in a PhD to help start the project. HEMP staff documented HEMP's operating systems and methods as if the organization would be duplicated. The team codified best practices and then invited mentors and mentees to review and edit the materials.

Mentor Lirel Holt violates all HEMP rules by kissing his mentee, Lois Brayfield.

Blues Brothers Lirel Holt and Brent Niemuth entertain the HEMPers.

The system included training, testing, and tracking components so HEMP could provide initial training to new mentors and mentees. HEMP staff could also view mentor/mentee participation and see potential problems early on.

Not everyone was excited about moving in this direction. Some preferred that HEMP remain more free form. But Lirel believed that no organization could survive long-term without institutionalizing its rules, standards, and purposes.

"There will always be room to add new information provided by the amazing expertise and wisdom of mentors, mentees, and staff," Lirel says.

Sharing the HEMP System

Because of Lirel Holt's vision, HEMP now has documentation on administrative systems, staff job descriptions, accounting methods, charts of accounts, forms, and everything a program administrator might need as a reference.

"I've watched HEMP go from startup to a sterling mentoring program," Lirel says. "HEMP can now share that program with other communities throughout the U.S. and around the globe."

Lirel's own business has improved from his involvement with HEMP.

"Each mentee reminds me of ways I can be a better business person," he says. "Being involved with HEMP has been one of the most wonderful experiences of my life."

CHAPTER 14

CREATING A MENTEE BOOT CAMP

"It took me a year to catch on to the mentoring process," one mentee commented.

That comment inspired a new look at how mentors and mentees begin their relationship.

"We have learned it is important to jumpstart the relationship and address key issues up front," says Ray Pitman, a long-time mentor and innovator at HEMP.

Getting the Main Issues on the Table

Initially, mentors and mentees stumbled through their first sessions.

Dan McDougal, a HEMP fellow and board president, has created a "boot camp" and designed an agenda for the first three months of meetings.

"There are half a dozen issues that most people have," Dan says. "During the first ninety days, we want to identify and address the entrepreneur's two main issues. Those two issues have probably been with the entrepreneurs their entire life."

Ray Pitman receives a giant watch for his giant service to HEMP.

New mentees fill out a SWOT (Strengths, Weaknesses, Opportunities, Threats) analysis before their first mentor meeting. This exercise jumpstarts the mentor/mentee relationship in several ways:

- Filling out the form helps mentees identify and articulate the types of assistance they need.
- Reading the SWOT analysis before their first meeting gives mentors a quick overview of the mentees issues and organization.
- Both can use the SWOT analysis to facilitate goal setting and to add structure to their early meetings.

"Using SWOT, we can also catch any challenges before they become too severe," Ray says.

Dan McDougal,
founder,
Dredge America

Reaching a Broader Understanding

The 360-degree assessment is another component of the boot camp. The mentor interviews a cross-section of the entrepreneur's employees and customers.

"Everyone in the world knows things about you and no one will tell you," Dan says. "Your employees are scared to be too direct. Friends don't want to hurt your feelings. Your mentor should say what no one else will tell you."

Offering Financial Analysis and Support

The boot camp includes another HEMP service: in-depth financial analysis. Entrepreneurs can be brilliant at sales, marketing, manufacturing, purchasing, and managing and still not know how to read a financial statement.

"Few entrepreneurs are accounting and finance people; that's usually not their strong suit." Dan says. "During the first meetings, we bring in the finance committee to review mentees' finances. That way they know where they stand and can project forward."

The financial team explains the statements and discusses the entrepreneur's accounting status. They discuss issues such as:

- Cash flow status.
- Growing the business by getting an outside investor (rarely recommended).
- Purchasing decisions.

For the first year, the financial people meet quarterly with each team of the mentees and mentors. Then they meet once a year, unless more is needed.

Swooping in for the Save

When a mentee has an urgent need, HEMP puts together a SWOT team to assist. For example, one mentee was struggling with a sales issue. The HEMP director brought in five mentors who were experts in sales. They worked with the mentee on her specific problem for several sessions.

Mentors have also assisted mentees who were in danger of losing their businesses. Through this extra assistance, HEMP has helped save a handful of companies.

Three happy campers: Faruk Capan, Sara Croke, and Adlai Kunst.

THE ECONOMICS OF HEMP:
MOVING TOWARDS SELF-SUSTAINABILITY

HEMP began with a sponsorship from University of Missouri-Kansas City as well as sponsorships and grants from the Kauffman Foundation and the Shirley & Barnett Helzberg Foundation. For years, the Helzberg Foundation underwrote HEMP.

Initially, HEMP was a work-in-progress and charged no fee for participation.

"As we proved HEMP offered significant value, we charged a fee so people would appreciate that value," says Walt Rychlewski. "Now, graduate mentees realize they need to support the organization financially, as well as with time and energies."

The organization is gradually moving towards self-sustainability. Here are some of the ways HEMP brings in funds.

Walt Rychlewski,
professor at the Bloch School of Business & School of Computing and Engineering, UMKC

Mentee Money

Entrepreneurs pay annual fees (in 2012 it was $4,000) to participate in the program. While this payment doesn't begin to cover the cost of all the services provided, it does engender increased commitment from the mentee.

Fees for Fellows

Many college graduates can't wait to be done with their training and be off on their own. But HEMP graduates often want to stay connected to the HEMP community. So HEMP Fellows emerged. For an annual fee (in 2012 it was $750), graduates and others can stay involved, attend programs and retreats, and serve on committees.

Gabe Kaniger enjoys a happy moment.

Skuli and Ginny Gudmundsson celebrate their success.

Leslie Tomlinson toasts Jay Tomlinson and Sam Meers.

"Fore" Fundraising

In 2002, HEMPer Melody Warren started a HEMP golf tournament, raising money through hole sponsorships and tournament fees.

"Originally the goal was to have fun and break even," says Christina Friederichs. "But the event now makes a profit."

Adlai Kunst and Steve Ward demonstrate the ultimate level of trust with fellow HEMPers, Dave Cacioppo and Mike O'Malley.

Mike Bryant, Melody Warren (golf tournament founder), Al Rickert, and Gerry Minor.

It "Ads" Up

"These local entrepreneurs are high on HEMP."

That was the headline for a HEMP ad in the local *KC Business Journal*. The original ad featured photos of fifteen HEMP entrepreneurs along with their business logos and generated a lot of visibility for the featured companies. HEMPers were willing to pay to be included in such advertising and graduate mentees paid $200 each to be featured in subsequent ads. This venture generated revenue and also brought in some new mentees.

Paying for the Free Lunch

From time to time, HEMP sponsored Lunch with the Big Guy (LWTBG), which offers a small group of mentees a chance to have a conversation and lunch with Barnett. Initially, HEMP paid for the program. Then one grateful graduate offered to sponsor a lunch. The idea caught on and now HEMPers sign up to sponsor a lunch, which they host at their businesses.

These sponsorships reduce a cost that HEMP was absorbing.

Advancing with Retreats

The yearly retreats offered an additional opportunity to generate revenue. Mentors don't pay but other attendees pay for the experience. HEMP generated as much as $10,000 profit from some retreats.

These local entrepreneurs are all high on HEMP.

Maybe that's because they averaged 43% revenue growth, 30% employee growth and contributed $748 million to the economy.

The impressive group of business leaders represented above, and over 200 others like them, have a reason to be high on success. They have access to an awe-inspiring network of local business icons to help them grow.

For each of the past 16 years, the Helzberg Entrepreneurial Mentoring Program (HEMP) has matched 10 to 15 passionate leaders of high potential companies (Mentees) with A-List, veteran business professionals (Mentors) from the Kansas City community. The time-tested matching process takes into account the strengths and weaknesses of Mentees and their desire to learn, along with their track record of success, to find a suitable Mentor to help guide them to the next level.

Are you ready to get high on your business? Join us.

HEMP
Expose. Empower. Excel.

*Over an eight year period.

The mentee class of 2007 presents HEMP with a generous donation.

Giving for Receiving

The initial donations to HEMP came from grateful mentors and mentees. One mentor donated $20,000 for the development of the HEMP website. Several graduates have donated $10,000 each for operating costs. A recent speaker at a HEMP retreat was so impressed with the program that he donated $10,000.

HEMP has a development committee that creates annual sponsorship levels and formalizes giving opportunities.

To keep HEMP moving forward, the 2011 president of HEMP, Ralph Wrobley, of counsel, Husch Blackwell, LLP, orchestrated a formal executive committee process, engaging the group in creating a strategic plan. All committees participated in their portion of the plan and the board is using that plan as a guideline.

The quest for self-sustainability continues as the team looks for additional fund-raising and funding opportunities.

Ralph Wrobley,
of counsel, Husch Blackwell, LLP

16

STARTING AN ENTREPRENEURIAL MENTORING PROGRAM

Institutionalizing HEMP

Characteristics of Long-Lived Organizations (Five Things to Strive For):

1. High Ethical and Performance Standards
2. Sensitive to All Environments
3. The Organization is Seen as a Community
4. Conservative Cash Management
5. Safe Experiments for Change Encouraged at the Periphery

If you want to create your own mentoring program:

- Survey local leaders and potential mentors to get their reaction to an entrepreneurial mentoring program.
- Look for people who have benefited from mentoring.
- Seek local businesses (long-distance relationships have not worked out).
- Search out those who have experience serving on boards or advisory committees.
- Seek out community or other foundations dedicated to building entrepreneurial excellence and innovation to offer funding opportunities.

Developing a Mentor/Mentee Program

- Create a structure that supports the mentoring relationship and process.
- Clarify the functions and limitations of the central office.
- Select a managing director who stays in contact with all participants and who reports to the board.
- Create working committees and other opportunities for graduates to stay involved so they'll continue to support the organization.
- Create fundraising and other revenue-generating events and opportunities.

What follows are some of the documents and forms that may be helpful. For further information, visit www.helzbergmentoring.org.

MENTOR'S BILL OF RIGHTS

To assure that the certified HEMP Mentor is satisfied with the merits and work expected from the Helzberg Entrepreneurial Mentoring Program and their Mentee, we declare that all Mentors have the following rights:

1. To have a full and open understanding of HEMP's mission and be adequately trained both prior to accepting the role of Mentor and on an ongoing basis.

2. To accept or reject a Mentee prior to or after being matched by HEMP.

3. To be respected by the organization's governing board, and to expect the board to exercise prudent judgment in its stewardship responsibilities.

4. To have access to HEMP staff in order to better assist in the Mentoring process.

5. To leave the program at any time if they determine they are not capable of assisting the Mentee in a professional and ethical manner.

6. To receive appropriate acknowledgment and recognition for their charitable efforts.

7. To have their contributions and counseling handled with respect and confidentiality by their Mentee.

8. To expect that all relationships with individuals representing the HEMP organization will be professional in nature.

9. To be informed by HEMP should any potential conflicts with the Mentee arise.

10. To have the opportunity to ask questions of the organization and receive prompt, truthful and forthright answers.

_____   _____
SIGNATURE   DATE

MENTEE'S BILL OF RIGHTS

To assure that the HEMP Mentee is satisfied with the merits and work expected from the Helzberg Entrepreneurial Mentoring Program and to appreciate the benefits of having a program and a Mentor to help them grow as a leader, we declare that all Mentees have the following rights:

1. To have a full and open understanding of HEMP's mission, the Mentoring program, and expectations of Mentees prior to accepting a Mentor.

2. To have regular access to their Mentor and HEMP staff coupled with ongoing training and support specifically for Mentees.

3. To be able to accept or reject a Mentor prior to being matched by HEMP.

4. To be respected by the organization's governing board, and to expect the board to exercise prudent judgment in its stewardship responsibilities.

5. To ask for a Mentor change or to leave the program at any time if they feel they are not being capably Mentored in a professional and ethical manner.

6. To receive appropriate acknowledgment and recognition for their participation in the program and their good efforts.

7. To have personal and business information handled with respect and confidentiality by their Mentor and any individual representing the HEMP program.

8. To expect that all relationships with individuals representing the HEMP organization will be professional in nature.

9. To be informed by HEMP should any potential conflicts with the Mentor arise.

10. To have the opportunity to ask questions of the organization and receive prompt, truthful and forthright answers.

_____   _____

SIGNATURE   DATE

HEMP MENTOR/MENTEE CODE OF CONDUCT
Directions: Please review and sign with your Mentor/Mentee

We understand that a HEMP mentoring relationship is a unique relationship that requires the highest standards of honesty, mutual trust, confidentiality and openness. Therefore _____ (the Mentee) and _____ (the Mentor) commit to the following:

All discussions and communications within the HEMP program and between the Mentor and Mentee, both written and oral, will be treated with the utmost integrity, confidentiality and high ethical standards; both parties understand that, unless specifically requested, no information obtained through this relationship shall be shared with anyone;

Both the Mentor and Mentee will make every attempt to respond to messages from HEMP parties, including staff and participants;

Mentee will be as forthcoming and open as the Mentee is able, knowing that the amount and depth of information provided directly relates to the success and productivity of the mentoring relationship; Mentee commits to providing an honest representation of issues and facts regarding any issue presented (i.e., Mentee agrees that, if warranted, Mentee will put his/her "worst foot forward");

Mentee understands that the primary means of learning is from feedback provided by Mentor, and other HEMP members if needed, and understands that the HEMP member providing his/her opinions, observations, direction and questions does so in the spirit of constructive critique;

Mentee has completed the on-line training regarding the HEMP program and understands the mission of the HEMP program;

Mentee commits to attend a minimum of 75% of HEMP events (excluding events described as "Bonus Events");

Mentor agrees to approach the mentoring relationship with an open mind and a willingness to learn how the Mentee's business operates, so as to provide real and constructive critique to Mentee;

Mentor agrees to respectfully challenge Mentee to exceed Mentee's own expectations and encourage Mentee to grow both personally and professionally;

Mentor understands that he/she has the right to ask questions in the pursuit of understanding the Mentee's business operations, but that the Mentee has the right to refuse to answer any questions without the need for explanation; Mentor agrees to assist in finding additional mentoring, if necessary, from other HEMP members should issues present themselves that Mentor feels are beyond the scope and experience of the Mentor;

Mentor understands that HEMP is a mentoring program and as such, commits to refrain from taking any business interest, either directly or indirectly, in Mentee's company for the entire term of the mentoring relationship; Should Mentee and Mentor mutually agree that Mentor shall take any such business interest, then before such arrangement is effected, Mentor shall notify the Managing Director of HEMP in writing of his/her withdrawal from the HEMP program;

Mentor commits to attend a minimum of 50% of HEMP events (excluding events described as "Bonus Events") but is encouraged to attend at least 75% of all such events;

During Mentee's first year in HEMP, Mentor and Mentee agree to meet at least two times per month and thereafter, at least one time per month for the duration of Mentee's participation in the HEMP program;

Mentor and Mentee agree to work together to try and resolve any issues that may present themselves as an impediment to an optimum mentoring relationship and understand that the HEMP Staff is available for assistance in such resolution at any time; However, if at any time, either the Mentor or Mentee should determine that the mentoring relationship is not an optimum one for any reason, either Mentor or Mentee should feel comfortable contacting the Managing Director of HEMP who will immediately review the situation and, depending on the availability of other Mentors/Mentees, rematch the Mentee in an attempt to achieve an optimum mentoring relationship;

Failure of either Mentor or Mentee to abide by the Code of Conduct presented above may result in removal from the HEMP program.

_____   _____

Mentee Signature   Printed Name

Date: _____

_____   _____

Mentor Signature   Printed Name

Date: _____

HEMP MENTOR/MENTEE "JUMPSTART" CHECKLIST
by Laura Laiben

General Observations From a Third-Year Mentee:

I am not the poster child for a perfect mentee. In fact, I wish I would have done some things differently. Anyway, you know what they say about hindsight…So I have come up with a list of information and documents that I would (and for many of these items… actually did) give to my mentor within the first few weeks. (Yes, this will take some time to put together…get over it! I wish I would have done it ALL right away.) Other more knowledgeable mentors and mentees will likely have additional and better ideas. This thought process might help in your compilation process…Pretend that your mentor is representing you and your business in a major purchase or lawsuit. What does she/he need to know about you and your company in order to represent you?

1. A copy of your entire HEMP application
2. A copy of your personality profile (HF4D)
3. A written description of your business
4. Current company marketing materials
   a. Brochures
   b. Business card
   c. Marketing packets to prospective clients/customers
   d. Current and a few past newsletters
   e. Whatever else you have and currently use to describe your business
5. Pictures of your company and/or product
6. Copies of articles, awards and news clippings about you and/or your company
7. An organizational chart for your company (hand-written on a napkin is better than nothing)
8. Directions to your office
9. Financial Statements for the past 3 years including a current Balance Sheet IN WHATEVER FORM THEY MAY EXIST (C'mon. You can do it! Breathe! Let it go!)
10. Tax Returns for the business for the past 3 years (ditto)
11. Set a date (maybe ½ day) for your mentor just to learn about your business – don't focus on problems – just get him/her educated
12. Within the first few months, read a couple of the books recommended by HEMP so you know the "lingo" (*Good to Great*, *The E-Myth*, whatever.)

> **THE LEAST YOU CAN DO:**
> *(For you competitive folks, this section is worth 100 "HEMP Points" and a pat on the back!)*

13. Any financial analyses that you may have completed to this point: charts, graphs, summaries, etc. that may help your mentor visualize your business better
14. Current Company Mission Statement (if you have one)
15. Current Personal Mission Statement (if you have one)
16. Top 10 Things I Think You Need to Know About Me to Have an Effective Mentor/Mentee Relationship (for we anal retentive types!)

> **IF YOU FEEL A BIT MORE INDUSTRIOUS:**
> *(Value: 1,000 "HEMP Points" and a hand-shake from Barnett)*

17. Description of your short and long term business goals
18. Description of your short and long term personal goals
19. Summary of employee benefits
20. Summary of insurance policies
21. Brief information about your family
22. Specific options for best times to meet regularly

IF YOU'RE MUCH FURTHER ALONG THAN MOST OF US AT THIS POINT!

(Showoff!)

23. Strategic plan for your business
24. Description of management philosophy
25. Description of business systems measurement tools
26. Business operation flowcharts
27. Company operations manuals
28. Summary of estate planning goals (or description of estate planning currently in place)
29. Business valuation analysis
30. Succinct description of current business challenges
31. A description of where you hope to be in one year as a result of your involvement in HEMP

Top 10 Things You Should Know About Me

Michelle Robin, Your Wellness Connection
September 2009

1. I am committed and on purpose for Wellness.
2. I tend to be skeptical and self-critical. I am a questioner; I ask a lot of questions and get too many opinions.
3. I love connecting people to resources.
4. I need to be held accountable and challenged.
5. I love educating and teaching.
6. I move fast and I think faster.
7. I live a double-edge sword; I am always on the Wellness, Spirituality, Marketing page and that is personal to most people. It is easy for me to never turn the page.
8. I see the big picture with attention to details.
9. I need someone with good boundaries of time and commitment.
10. I believe intuition is one of the most important skills to develop in your business.

A GOOD MENTOR STRIVES TO BE

An active listener	A giver of options, not directions
Available	Honest
A challenger	A networker
A cheerleader	An objective sounding board
Committed to helping	Open-minded
Empathetic	Passionate
Enthusiastic	Patient
A facilitator	Proactive
Focused	Respectful

A GOOD MENTEE STRIVES TO BE

Adaptable	Honest about successes and failures
Available	Humble
Committed	Involved
Consistent in providing feedback	Not defensive
Curious	Proactive
Flexible	Realistic in expectations
Focused	Receptive
A good questioner	Responsive
A good listener	

HEMP DICTIONARY

DEFINITIONS

As with any good entrepreneurial organization, we don't rely on Webster, but invent our own.

Advisory Board – a nonlegal sounding board of trusted advisers with no pecuniary or family attachments who will bluntly evaluate policies, goals, and new directions for the company.

Alumni – any mentee who has graduated from the HEMP program.

Anniversary Talks – yearly meeting between the HEMP managing director and the mentee to discuss program issues, their successes and failures over their three-year period, and the lessons they have learned.

Board of Directors – a group consisting of the Executive Committee and the chairpersons of each committee. The board, through various committee chairs, brings about new and innovative approaches to consistently improve HEMP. They work with HEMP staff to execute the organization's mission.

Confidentiality – defined within the organization as total nondisclosure of information to any member or nonmember without permission.

Counselors – individuals who are qualified to be mentors but are not matched with a mentee.

Community – the unified body of individuals which is the core of HEMP.

Educational Sessions – ongoing educational programs which cover five major categories: Sales, Marketing, Finance, Operations, and People issues, such as leadership, management, and human resources.

Executive Committee – a group consisting of the chairman of the board, vice chairman of the board, the current president, president-elect, and two other members appointed by the committee not exceeding seven people. The Executive Committee meets monthly and sets strategy and policy for the organization.

Fellows – graduate mentees who have elected to stay active in HEMP, serving as committee chairs, board members, participating in SWOT teams and special assignments related to helping mentees. This group also hosts graduate classes to further improve their own companies, as well as programs on how to help others.

Forum Groups – groups of eight to twelve participants who meet monthly and provide a consistent, structured, small group support environment.

Friends of HEMP – those who give generously to the program.

Graduation – annual ceremony at the end of the three-year managed mentoring program. (Many of these relationships become permanent.)

HEMP – Helzberg Entrepreneurial Mentoring Program.

HEMPer – a participant of HEMP.

Lunch with the Big Guy (LWTBG) – lunches with six to eight members and the founder to discuss personal or company issues in a totally confidential atmosphere.

Matching Process – the matching of mentees and mentors.

Mentee – an entrepreneur seeking growth who is willing to commit to the formalized three-year HEMP program by working one-on-one with a mentor for guidance and coaching on how to develop as a leader in order to enhance the business.

Mentee Boot Camp – designed to help jumpstart the mentee/mentor relationship, including an agenda to be used during their first three months of meeting, a 360-degree assessment, and in-depth financial analysis.

Mentee Selection Committee – a group within HEMP that reviews mentee applications and determines who qualifies for a site visit. This group also makes the mentor-mentee match.

Mentor – a seasoned, veteran business owner who is willing to share his or her experience with an entrepreneur who seeks knowledge in areas in which they have yet to be exposed, empowering them to excel as entrepreneurs.

Networking – establishes mutually beneficial relationships among HEMPers and for which time is allotted at every HEMP event.

Pay It Forward – a committee of people focused on gathering donations for the sustainability of HEMP.

Goodie bag for the 2008 retreat.

Putting Your Worst Foot Forward – sharing information about failures and challenges, not just successes and triumphs, in order to benefit the most from a mentoring relationship.

Quarterly Conversations – conversations initiated by the HEMP managing director to the mentees to specifically inquire about challenges but also to build a relationship with them and act as a resource.

Retreats - one-day getaways that provide opportunities to learn from business leaders about topics of mutual interest.

Site Visit – a visit to the prospective mentee's place of business to view operations and interact with the candidate.

Speed-Matching Event – an event held for new mentees and available mentors where each mentee visits with selected mentors and picks three prioritized choices of mentors. Similarly, each mentor picks three top prioritized choices.

Supporter – graduate mentees and others who wish to support HEMP financially and continue to receive news of HEMP's happenings. This membership also includes the privilege of attending the annual meeting.

SWOT Analysis – study submitted by mentees of their business's Strengths, Weaknesses, Opportunities, and Threats.

SWOT Team – a small group of four to six people who come together on an as-needed basis to assist other HEMPers with a specific issue. This is generally a one- or two-time meeting. The HEMPer requests the meeting through the HEMP staff, who facilitate with various committee chairs to identify and bring together the SWOT team.

Three Magic Questions – What are we doing that you like? What are we doing that you don't like? What are we not doing that you would like?

UDM – Ultimate Decision Maker, which is one of the criteria needed to be selected as a mentee.

The visiting squad Walt Rychlewski, Ray Pitman, Barnett, Lirel Holt, Christina Friederichs, and Ralph Wrobley travel to meet potential mentees.

Robert B. Cialdini, Ph.D., *Influence*: *The Psychology of Persuasion*. New York: HarperBusiness, 2006.

Robert B. Cialdini, Noah J. Goldstein, Steve J. Martin, *Yes! 50 Scientifically Proven Ways to Be Persuasive*. New York: Free Press, 2008.

Jim Collins, *Good to Great: Why Some Companies Make the Leap...and Others Don't*. New York: HarperCollins, 2001.

Ted Cohn, *Management Smarts: Listen Think Act*. (To order, send check for $12, postage included, to Ted Cohn, 923 Fifth Avenue 4A, New York, NY 10021-2649.)

Michael Gerber, *The E-Myth Revisited: Why Most Small Businesses Don't Work and What to Do about It*. New York: HarperCollins, 1995.

Barnett C. Helzberg Jr., *What I Learned Before I Sold to Warren Buffett*. Hoboken, N.J.: John Wiley & Sons, 2003.

Tony Hsieh, CEO, Zappos.com, Inc., *Delivering Happiness: A Path to Profits, Passion, and Purpose*. New York: Business Plus, 2010.

Dr. Pierre Mornell, *45 Effective Ways for Hiring Smart: How to Predict Winners & Losers in the Incredibly Expensive People-Reading Game*. Berkeley, CA: Ten Speed Press, 2001.

A

Advisory Boards, 11, 45, 46, 77, 93, 95, 122, 123, 142
Amirahmadi, Elizabeth, *23*, 48-52, *133*
Anniversary Talks, 121, 142
Antequera, Carlos, *133*

B

Beller, Jay, *117*, *133*
Benner, Dick, 45, *47*, 109-111
Bennett, Bob, *116*
Bloch, Henry, *2*, *3*, *4*, *6*, *7*, 90-92
Bloch, Tom, *92*
Brayfield, Lois, *85*, *125*
Brush, Bob, *98*
Bryant, Mike, *131*
Burcham, Grant, 40, 41

C

Cacioppo, Dave, 80-83, *130*
Capan, Faruk, *128*
Cates, Jeff, *116*, *117*
Clark, Maxine, 117
Cofield, Leanne, 108-111
Cohn, Ted, *2*, 77, 122, 145
Cohn, Alice, *122*
Collene, Jason, 62-65, *133*
Corby, *8*
Counselors, 11, 142
Croke, Sara, 82, *128*

D

Davis, James, 96-99
Davis, Rich, 3
Defining Mentors, 15
Defining the Entrepreneurial Mentee, 14, 15
Dole, Bob, 72

E

Eddy, Bill, *2*, *3*, *8*, *9*, 10, 11, 15, 26, *42*, 113, 114, 121
Educational Sessions, 9, 142
Epsten, Bob, *117*
Ervin, Janene, *133*
Executive Committee, 133, 142

F

Fellows, 10, 50, 129, 142
Forums, 10, 142
French, Bill, 3
Friederichs, Christina, 8, *19*, *91*, *117*, 118, 120, 121, 130, *144*

G

Gudmundsson, Ginny, *130*
Gudmundsson, Skuli, *130*

H

Hagen, Alton, *10*
Hamilton, Mindy, *91*
Hartnett, Bill, 12
Hayhow, Jack, *87*
Helzberg, Barnett, *1*, *2*, *3*, *5*, *9*, 50, 72, 73, 75-78, 89, 90, 93, 95, 104-106, *116*, *117*, *118*, 124, 131, *133*, 139, *144*, 145
Helzberg, Bush, 9, *116*
Helzberg, Charley, *93*
Helzberg Foundation, 4, 129
Helzberg, Shirley Bush, *3*, *116*, *117*
HEMP Ad, 131, *132*
HEMP Mentor/Mentee Code of Conduct, 137, 138
HEMP Mentor/Mentee "Jumpstart" Checklist, 139, 140
Hesse, Sue, *10*

Hoffman, Chuck, *1*, 2, 4, 14, *95*, *103*, *117*, *118*
Hoffman, Ellene, *95*, *116*
Holt, Lirel, *59*, *118*, 124-126, *144*
Holt, Sharon, *59*
Homoly, Andrew, 104-107

I

J

Jackson, Stuart, *118*, *133*
Jacoby, Mary Lou, 25-28, 58, *85*
Jones, Laura Lee, *9*, 16-20
Julian, Kay, *41*, 112-115

K

Kaniger, Gabe, *87*, *129*
Karbank, Barney, *3*, 4, *13*
Kauffman Foundation, 4, 91, 129
Ketcham, Ernie, 44-47
Ketcham, Kitty, *47*
King, Scott, *133*
Klink, Cheryl, *12*
Klink, Doug, *9*, *12*
Koehler, Kathy, *117*
Krska, Rick, 75-79, *86*
Kunst, Adlai, *128*, *130*
Kushnir, Paul, *117*
Kushnir, Shannah, *117*

L

Laiben, Laura, 39-43, *118*, 139
Lieberman, Joe, 21-24, *133*
Livers, Deuce, 57-61
Livers, Lenda, *59*
Long, Peter, *12*
Love, Bill, 53-55
Love, Missy, 53-56
Lunch with the Big Guy (LWTBG), *9*, 50, 72, 106, 131, 143

M

McDonnell, Tom, *9*
McDougal, Dan, 34-38, 63, 64, *82*, 98, *117*, 127, 128
McDougal, Renee, *10*, 37, 117
Meers, Sam, *98*, *130*

Mentee Selection Committee, 118, 119, 121, 143
Mentee's Bill of Rights, 136
Mentor's Bill of Rights, 135
Mentoring Program Guidelines, 141
Minor, Gerry, *131*
Minor, Judy, *117*
Murray, Ted, 105, 106

N

Nelson, Ed, *14*
Networking, 2, 8, 9, 11, 15, 59, 79, 118, 119, 143
Niemuth, Brent, *126*
Nilsen, Dan, *9*, *102*
Nixon, Bob, *116*

O

O'Malley, Mike, *9*, 40, 81, *117*, *130*
O'Neill, Danny, 7, *78*, 89-95

P

Pacumbaba-Watson, Gina, *116*, *133*
Pasley, Mike, *14*
Pitman, Ray, *1*, 21-23, 31, 32, 36, 37, 57, 58, 60, 62, 63, *117*, *118*, 127, *144*
Proffer, Don, *6*, *117*
Proffer, Molly, *6*
Putting the worst foot forward, 5, 12, 42, 109, 137, 143

Q

Quarterly Conversations, 120, 121, 143

R

Rashid, Dawn Eddy, *117*
Rashid, Ken, 17, 18
Rawlings, Jason, *133*
Reisler, Bill, 101, 102
Retreats, 9, 12, 106, 114, 129, 131, 144
Rickert, Al, *131*
Robin, Michelle, *19*, 83, 100-103, 140
Runyan, Joe, 66-70
Rychlewski, Walt, 5, 6, 8, *118*, 129, *144*

S

Schaffer, Tim, *87*
Shapiro, Bob, 49, *50*
Sharma, Neal, 71-74
Short, Gary, 29-33
Short, Teresa, *32*
Site Visit, 105, 118, 119, 143, 144
Sladkey, Jack, *117*, *118*
Sladkey, Lois, *117*
Smith, Nancy, *14*
Sosland, Morton, 2, 4
Spears, Mark, *116*
Stuelke, Gina, *116*
Stuelke, Jim, *133*
Sullivan, Bob, *87*
SWOT Analysis, 68-70, 127, 144
SWOT Teams, 10, 22, 23, 63, 128, 142, 144

T

Taylor, Linda Gill, 9, *10*, 76, 77
Thomas, Dr. Harvey, *1*, 2, *116*
Tomlinson, Jay, *116*, *130*
Tomlinson, Leslie, *130*

U

V

Vandewalle, John, 9, *82*
Voth, Emily, 84-88

W

Ward, Steve, *130*
Warren, Melody, *41*, 68, *116*, 130, 131
Womack, Cheryl, 72
Wrobley, Ralph, 133, *144*

X

Y

Yennie, Richard, 101
Young, Deborah, *11*, *14*, 119
Young President's Organization (YPO), 2, 76

Z

Zecy, Mark, *10*

Share your story!

If you are an entrepreneur with a story about how you were mentored or how you mentored someone else, we would love to hear from you. Send your story to info@helzbergmentoring.org. Selected stories can be viewed at www.helzbergmentoring.org.